DEADLY EMILY

Kathy Lee

© Kathy Lee 1998, 2010
First published 1998, this edition 2010
ISBN 978 1 84427 394 2

Scripture Union
207–209 Queensway, Bletchley, Milton Keynes, MK2 2EB
Email: info@scriptureunion.org.uk
Website: www.scriptureunion.org.uk

Scripture Union Australia
Locked Bag 2, Central Coast Business Centre, NSW 2252
Website: www.scriptureunion.org.au

Scripture Union USA
PO Box 987, Valley Forge, PA 19482
Website: www.scriptureunion.org

British Library Cataloguing-in-Publication Data
A catalogue record of this book is available from the British Library.

Printed and bound in India by Thomson Press India Ltd

Cover design: Martin Lore
Cover illustration: Simon Rumble

Scripture Union is an international charity working with churches in more than 130 countries, providing resources to bring the good news of Jesus Christ to children, young people and families and to encourage them to develop spiritually through the Bible and prayer.

As well as our network of volunteers, staff and associates who run holidays, church-based events and school Christian groups, we produce a wide range of publications and support those who use our resources through training programmes.

To Sylvie Prouse, with thanks for all her encouragement

CHAPTER 1

DEADLY EMILY

I bet you think I can't even spell. I bet you think the name of this book should be "Deadly Enemy", not Emily. Well, you're wrong.

It was Gran who mentioned her first. I was leaning my elbows on the window sill, staring at the rain; not because I like rain, but because there is zero to do in Brilby on a wet day. Gran says Brilby is the third wettest village in England.

I said, "Gran, are there any other kids in Brilby? Any my age, I mean?"

Gran paused in her knitting. "There's the Preston boys – no, they'd be older than you – and then there's that red-haired Smith girl. Now that's a funny thing... if I'm not mistaken, her name's the same as yours. Just fancy! Two Emily Smiths in the same village."

I thought about this. For some reason it made me feel strange – sort of prickly – as if a stranger had been writing in my private diary. But that was silly; it was only a name.

"Perhaps we're related somehow," I said.

Gran snorted. "Not very likely, is it? Your dad's family were all from down south. And anyway Smith's a common name – common as muck."

Gran's name is Mrs Thistlethwaite, which sounds like a sneeze. Smith is a much more sensible name, I think. And I wondered what Mum would call herself after the divorce was made final. Would she still be Mrs Smith?

"We might be in the same class at school, that Emily and me; could be a bit confusing." There had been another Emily at my old school, but our surnames were different. Although she hadn't been a special friend of mine, I suddenly longed to see her again, to see my old school, and all my friends, and even the teachers... I might never set eyes on any of them again.

Instead I was starting at a new school where I wouldn't know anyone at all, not even my big brother Tom. Brilby is too small to have a school so we would have to go by bus to Caston, five miles away. I would be in the junior school and Tom would be in the seniors.

I was dreading it. I tried to persuade Mum that we could stay away from school. After all, we weren't going to be in Brilby for long. Staying with Gran was just a temporary thing, in between selling our house in London and deciding where to live next.

"But that might take months," Mum said. "You can't spend all that time away from school; you'd get behind with your work. And you'd be bored to death. And anyway, it's illegal."

"What's illegal – being bored to death? They'd better arrest the whole population of Brilby, then." Tom gave a huge yawn.

Mum said, "Oh come on. It isn't that bad. You used to love coming here on holiday."

"But that was in the summer, Mum. It's January now, or hadn't you noticed? It's pouring with rain, and we don't know anybody, and Gran hasn't even got a decent telly."

"Or a computer."

"Or a book less than a hundred years old."

"Or a football. Or a DVD player. Or a bed without lumps in."

"Sshh! You'll hurt Gran's feelings," said Mum. "Now look, I know this isn't easy for either of you. But things will be better when we get settled somewhere. We'll be able to unpack all our own things then, and feel more at home. But there just isn't the space at the moment, is there?"

This was true. Gran's house was only small, and it was crammed so full of furniture that there was hardly any room for people. Tom had to sleep on a camp bed in the attic, among the boxes and dusty piles of books. Mum and I slept in the spare room; the bed smelt of mothballs.

The worst thing was having no peace and quiet – no place that was mine. If I wanted to read quietly in the bedroom Mum would come in to sort out the washing, or Tom would want to rummage in the cases.

"What are you reading?"

"Oh, nothing." And I would push the book under my pillow.

What I was reading was my Bible. (My family thought this habit was weird, but probably harmless.) It was a new Bible, a leaving present from the St Mark's Mob – the Sunday night group at my church in London. There were some notes to help you read a few verses each day. So far I had managed to do it every day... well, almost.

Sometimes the readings were boring, but sometimes I came across a verse that might have been written just for me. I wrote down the good ones on the blank page at the front of the book:

God will cover you with his wings; you will be safe in his care.

Or my all-time favourite:

If I flew away beyond the east
or lived in the farthest place in the west
he would be there to lead me,
he would be there to help me.

Beyond the east... farthest west... that must include even Brilby. Mustn't it?

But every day I prayed the same thing: *please, please make Mum and Dad get together again. Then we can all go home.*

CHAPTER 2

THE GANG OF FOUR

Monday came too quickly - Black Monday, the day we started school.

It began badly. There was yet another letter for Mum, telling her she hadn't got a job she'd applied for. She ripped it up, threw it in the bin and started yelling at us.

"All right, Mum," Tom said. "Not my fault, is it? If they'd asked me, I'd have made you managing director."

She laughed then. "I'd settle for being the managing director's secretary, or anybody's secretary. Hurry up! You'll miss your bus."

Tom and I went out into the grey winter daylight. At least it wasn't raining for once.

Waiting for the bus was a boy who looked about Tom's age, and a girl. Was this the other Emily Smith? And could we be friends? I looked her over cautiously. She was skinny and sharp-faced, with hair as red as a fire engine. I saw she was wearing school uniform in a horrible shade of sludge green.

"Oh no, that makes it even worse," I muttered. "We'll be the only ones not wearing uniform – everybody will know we don't belong."

The red-haired girl was doing up her shoelace when the bus arrived, so it happened that we got on before her. And that was the start of a whole busload of trouble. If only I'd known!

The bus was almost empty. Tom and I sat down on the back seat. Next thing I knew, the red-haired girl was standing there, glaring at us.

"You can't sit there. That's our seat," she said.

The way she said it – as if she owned the entire bus company – got right up my nose. If she'd been polite, maybe we would have been polite too. Instead, Tom said in an American gangster voice, "Oh yeah? Who says?"

"It's our seat. We always sit here, every day. Why can't you go somewhere else?"

"Because," Tom said lazily, "we got here first."

This made her face go scarlet with fury. The colour clashed badly with her hair. Was it really true that red hair went with a fiery temper?

"You never," she said. "I was at the front of the queue until you pushed past."

I said, "We didn't push past. You were tying your shoe. Anyway, this is silly. There's room for all of us."

"Not when my mates get on; there won't be." She slammed herself down at the far end of the seat.

At the next village another girl got on and sat next to her. They talked in whispers; we ignored them. The bus was filling up and getting noisier. Another stop, and two more of the gang got on. They had to sit on the seat in front. It was plain that they didn't like it.

Now we were coming to the outskirts of Caston. Soon Tom would get off, and I would be left on my own, one against four. I told myself it was babyish to feel scared.

The bus stopped outside the Senior School. Instead of saying goodbye to Tom, I got up and followed him towards the front of the bus, where I found an empty seat.

"Bye then. Hope you get on OK," I said in a small voice.

He grinned at me. "Don't fret yourself, looove," he said, trying to sound like Gran. "Always remember, worse things happen at sea – whatever that means." Then he was off, mixing with the crowds going through the school gates. Before the bus moved on, he was out of sight.

I felt alone and helpless. Looking round once, I saw the Gang of Four all together on the back seat, giggling about something. Probably the something was me.

We had done the bus trip with Mum the Saturday before, so I knew where to get off. She had offered to come to school with me that Monday, but I'd said no –

after all, I wasn't a 5-year-old. Now, I wished she had come with me after all. I would even have held her hand.

Instead I stood all by myself in the noisy playground. It was a nice playground, I had to admit, with trees and climbing frames, and even a grassy games pitch. Not like my London school, with its small tarmac square where there was hardly room to move. But at least I had friends there. Here, even in the middle of a crowd, I was quite alone.

Suddenly I remembered something: *beyond the east... farthest west... God would be there to help me.*

I took a deep breath and felt braver. Then the bell rang and I went in.

CHAPTER 3

CALLING NAMES

"Cheer up, love," said the driver, as I dragged myself onto the bus after school. "It may never happen."

"It's happening already," I muttered.

I sat down near the front of the bus. Nobody sat with me. The Enemy's gang went past me, laughing and pushing. One of them swung her bag and hit me on the shoulder. She giggled.

We stopped at the Senior School and I looked longingly for Tom. But when he got on, he hardly even said hello. He was talking to another boy. They sat behind me discussing Chelsea and Man United all the way back to Brilby.

It wasn't fair. Tom seemed to have found a friend already; I had only found an enemy. The whole day had been a disaster.

To begin with, there was the teacher, Mrs Bell. She was short and plump, with grey hair and a worried expression. She reminded me of Gran - elderly, rather fussy and easily flustered.

That morning, she stood me by her desk for everyone to stare at. I looked around. Oh no, the gang from the bus were all there: one, two, three, four.

"This is the new girl I told you about last week," she said. (Exactly what had she told them?) "Her name is Emily Smith. Yes. Another one!"

That made the red-haired girl jump to attention. She stared at me as if I was something nasty she'd just trodden in.

"Now Emily, where shall I put you? I know. You can be on the same table as Emily – I mean, our own Emily. As you share the same name, you ought to get on like a house on fire."

The other Emily smiled a sickly smile, a yes-miss, keep-well-in-with-teacher smile. I felt I would rather share a table with Count Dracula on a night of full moon.

Everyone shuffled up to make room for me. Seven faces stared at me; none looked particularly friendly.

"Now then, our main topic this term is the Roman Empire. How much do you know about the Romans, Emily?"

She was looking at me. My mind was a blank.

"Er... they lived in Rome?"

Everyone sniggered. Mrs Bell gave me a look that said: NO COMEDIANS IN MY CLASSROOM. "I can see you may have some catching up to do, Emily."

The other Emily put her hand up. She said in a smarmy voice, "Please, Mrs Bell, don't you think we could get a bit confused, two of us with the same name? How will we know who you're talking to?"

Mrs Bell frowned at me through her glasses.

"Perhaps we could call you by your middle name, if you have one." I shook my head frantically, but she was already looking in the register, where my name had been pencilled in. "Emily Maud Smith. Yes, let's call you Maud, shall we?"

One or two people giggled. I could feel my face getting red. "Please, Miss..."

"Yes, Maud? And by the way, I am not 'Miss'. My name is Mrs Bell."

"Er... it's just that I don't like my middle name much."

"You don't like the name Maud? I think it's a beautiful name. It's even in a famous poem: 'Come into the garden, Maud, for the black bat Night has flown...'"

How could I explain? Maud was not a beautiful name; it was silly and old and out of date. It was Gran's name. "I just don't like that name. I like my own name."

Mrs Bell looked put out. She asked the class for ideas, and got lots of suggestions.

"They could be Emily I and Emily II."

"No, that's daft; it sounds like a film title."

"We could say old Emily and new Emily."

"Thin Emily and fat Emily," said one of the girls from the bus. That was unfair. The other Emily was certainly thin – skinny even – but I'm not fat.

"Our Emily could use her middle name," said another girl.

Mrs Bell said, "I don't think there's any point in trying to change our Emily's name. We would never remember. We've all known her for too long. As for you..." she looked at me with active dislike, "...as you're only here on a temporary basis, I think you should choose a different name. Any name you like. After all it will only be for a few weeks."

I stared at the floor.

"Come on, choose a name for yourself. Otherwise we'll have to call you Maud."

"Denise," I said quickly. Denise was my best friend in London.

"Very well, Denise it shall be. Now then, we must get on; we've wasted enough time this morning."

She gave me some writing books. I wrote EMILY SMITH in big letters, then crossed out Emily as faintly as I could and wrote "Denise" in tiny writing.

At break time I asked someone where the toilets were. She sent me in the wrong direction, probably on purpose. Another girl rescued me. I vaguely recognised her from my new class.

She told me her name was Jenny. She seemed quite friendly and we went out to the playground together. But there, lying in wait, was Emily's gang.

"Oh look, it's Maud," one of them shouted.

"Maud, Maud! Come into the garden, the bats have flown away."

"She's batty, if you ask me. She's mad! Mad Maud!"

They gathered around in a tight little ring. I looked around for help, but there wasn't any. Jenny had walked away as soon as the gang came along.

"We don't want you here. Why did you come?"

"Yeah, go back where you came from."

"I didn't ask to come here," I said. "Do you think I'd choose to come to a rubbish school in a dead-end town like this? I'm going back to London the moment I can."

"Listen to her! She thinks she's so posh."

"Say something else, Maud."

"Mad Maud! Mad Maud!"

I tried to keep my voice steady, although I was shaking with fury. "My name is not Maud. It's Emily Smith."

"No it isn't. *I'm* Emily Smith," said the other Emily. "I was here first."

We stared at each other. If it came to a fight I would probably win – she was smaller and skinnier than me – but I couldn't beat all of them.

The weather saved me – for just then it started to rain. Brilliant rain! Excellent rain! We spent the rest of break indoors, and the lunch hour too. Nothing much could happen indoors; the dinner ladies kept an eye on things.

I said a silent thank you. But then I thought: *why doesn't God stop the bullying in the first place? Why doesn't he make it so that people have to be nice to each other?*

No answer came. I sat in the book corner all by myself, pretending to read.

CHAPTER 4

JUST LIKE OLD TIMES

Somehow I struggled through to the end of the week. One thing kept me going – at the weekend Dad was coming to see us. He phoned us quite often, but we hadn't actually seen him for weeks.

Dad wasn't going to sleep at Gran's house. "Over my dead body," said Gran. "What's wrong with Mrs Mabbutt's Bed and Breakfast place? He can stop there. I'm not having him in this house."

Mum sighed. "We're trying to keep things friendly. It's only a divorce, not World War Three."

"Friendly? There's nothing friendly about what he's done to you, is there? Going off and leaving you; moving in with that woman of his and leaving these poor children without a dad..."

I said fiercely, "He hasn't left us without a dad. He's still our dad."

"Not much good to you down in London, is he?"

I wanted to say: look, it's not Dad's fault that he's far away. Blame Mum; she's the one who dragged us here!

But I kept my mouth shut. I know when to do that – unlike Gran.

I hadn't told Mum just how bad things were at school. I tried to, once, but she wasn't really listening. She was filling in another form about a job. These days she was always anxious about something, usually money. I didn't want to add to her worries.

I did tell Tom about it, though. He got mad and started to think of all the things he would say to Emily and her friends on the bus. But I stopped him. If he annoyed the gang, it would be worse for me later when he'd gone.

***

Oh, it was great to see Dad again, even though he could only stay till Sunday night. The weekend went past far too quickly.

On Saturday it poured with rain, but that didn't matter because Dad had the car. We went to the bowling alley in Caston – just Dad, Tom and me. (Dad and Mum were being polite to each other in a cold sort of way; you couldn't describe them as friendly. As for Gran, she didn't smile once, the whole weekend.)

On Sunday, amazingly, it wasn't raining. Dad said that as we were out in the country we might as well get some air in our lungs, so we got well wrapped up and went for a walk over the moors. We had lunch in a country pub.

It was just like the old days, except that Mum wasn't with us.

I like it up there on the moors. You can see for miles. On the horizon are the hills of the Lake District, all heaped up like a crumpled duvet. Gran says if you can see them clearly it means there's rain on the way – and if you can't, it's already raining. The first time she said this I thought it was meant to be a joke.

Now, as we were coming back down into the valley, the view disappeared behind the long shoulder of the moor. Ahead of us was Brilby, with its slate-grey roofs and smoking chimneys.

Tom said, "Who on earth decided to build a village away out here?"

"It was a mining village once," Dad said. "But the mines packed up donkey's years ago. Your gran could tell you all about it. She always said she could write a book on the history of Brilby."

"Yeah, I bet she could. But who'd want to read it?" said Tom.

Nearly there; I found myself walking slower and slower – not wanting the afternoon to end.

"You're very quiet today, Emily," Dad said. "Are you OK?"

I wasn't OK. I was feeling lousy, partly because it was school next day, and partly because Dad was going back to London. But what was the point of saying so?

"Are you all right? Tom, is your sister all right? She seems to have gone dumb."

"She's always been dumb," I expected him to say, but he didn't. He said, "Tell him about the Enemy."

"No!"

"If you won't, I will. Dad, Emily's being bullied at school. There's this gang..."

And then it all came out, the whole story. The time they tried to lock me in the toilets; the time they tipped all my sandwiches out in the street; the time Emily knocked me over and then Mrs Bell told me off for being clumsy.

"It's not fair, the teacher's on their side too. She doesn't like me – she won't call me by my proper name. I'm supposed to be called Denise now, but I keep forgetting, so she shouts at me for not paying attention. I hate that school, I hate it!"

"Right," said Dad. "We'll see about this!"

He sounded so fierce that for a moment I felt hopeful. But what could he do, when he was going back to London that night?

What he did was have a blazing row with Mum. How that was supposed to help me, I don't know.

"I told you it was a bad move, taking the kids all the way up here, but you wouldn't listen. You should have stayed in London and kept them at their old schools."

"Oh yes? And where were we supposed to live? In a cardboard box?"

"You could have rented a place, couldn't you?"

"On the money you're giving me? You're joking. What you're giving me wouldn't pay the rent on a rabbit hutch."

They went on and on. It was the kind of row they used to have all the time, before they split up. (I timed them once – they rowed for three-and-a-half hours without stopping.)

Dad said, "What gets me is that you didn't even know she was unhappy. Don't you listen to your own daughter?"

"You're a fine one to talk. When did you ever listen to your daughter? You were never there when she needed you. You even forgot her birthday!"

On, and on, and on. I crept upstairs, but in Gran's small house I couldn't escape from their angry voices.

The row ended in the usual way, with Dad walking out. He slammed the door, jumped in the car and drove off. Watching from the bedroom window, I waved, but he didn't see me.

I went slowly back downstairs. Gran was making a cup of tea.

"Good riddance to bad rubbish," she said. "You're better off without him, love; believe me."

I wanted to hit her. No, I wanted to hit Emily. The weekend was ruined – and it was all Emily's fault.

CHAPTER 5

TWO AGAINST ONE

The next day, Mum went to see Mrs Bell after school. She came out looking serious.

"She says she'll keep an eye on those girls and make sure they leave you alone. But Emily..."

"What?"

"She says your own attitude isn't helping. She says you're a troublemaker."

"See! I told you she's on their side! She hates me!"

"No, she doesn't *hate* you, but she says you don't pay much attention in class. She says if she tells you off, you're sometimes cheeky. Is that true?"

I didn't answer.

Mum sighed. "Look, love, I know you don't want to be here, but it's not Mrs Bell's fault, is it? Don't take it out on her. You've got to help her if you want her to help you."

So I did try – I really did try. Mrs Bell didn't like me any better, though. I could hear it in her voice whenever she spoke to me.

It was strange. At my old school I was one of the clever ones in the class, but not any more. Nothing I did seemed to be right. The teacher thought I was a thicko; the rest of the class thought so too. Emily's gang started calling me "Dense" instead of Denise.

But they only did that when there were no grown-ups around. Mum's talk with Mrs Bell actually did some good, because two days later we had a whole assembly all about bullying, how evil it was and how all the staff were watching for any signs of it.

After that the gang left me alone for a bit – at least in public. They lay in wait for me in the toilets, of course, and at the bus stop going home. I began to avoid the toilets at break; I went during lesson time instead. Mrs Bell looked at me suspiciously. What did she think I would do? Have a quick fag? Steal the loo paper?

The girl called Jenny, who had talked to me on my first day, gradually got more friendly. She was quite shy and hard to talk to, not the kind of friend I would once have chosen, but better than nothing.

She was scared to death of Emily. If any of the gang so much as looked at her she would shrink away like a dog that expects to be beaten.

"Because it was me they used to pick on all the time," she told me.

I said, "How did you get them to stop? What's the secret?"

"Don't know. When you came, they started on you and forgot about me. They've always got to have somebody to have a go at. Before it was me, they used to pick on this girl called Louise, but she left."

"Oh, great! So I've got to wait until some other poor idiot comes along and takes over from me. It's not fair! There must be something I can do..."

Jenny surprised me by saying, "Well, you did do one thing right."

"What?"

"Told your dad. I was always too scared to tell anybody – I thought that lot would find out and beat me up. I used to make out I was ill so I could bunk off school."

That last idea had crossed my mind, but I didn't say so.

"Doesn't your mum think it's funny you've got better suddenly?" I asked.

"Yeah, she has noticed. She thinks it's the vitamin pills she got me. Disgusting, they are... they taste like sweets gone mouldy."

"You tell her it wasn't the pills that cured you. It was me, Emily Smith, the world-famous doctor! After I arrived, you were never ill again."

She giggled. "I did tell Mum about you, and she said..." Her voice trailed off into silence, and I looked round for enemies approaching. But no, it wasn't that. "She said would you like to come over after school one day?" Jenny said, not looking at me. You could tell she expected the answer to be no.

So of course I said yes. I quite enjoyed it, and later I asked Mum if Jenny could come around one Saturday. Mum looked pleased. "I'm glad you've made a friend," she said.

"She's not a friend. She's just someone I hang around with at school."

All the same I was glad to see her. Saturdays had got even more boring lately, because Tom was never there. He always went off to Preston's Farm to see his friend Matthew.

"What's so wonderful about a farm?" I asked him.

"It's interesting – seeing lambs being born, driving a tractor..."

"You drive a tractor?"

"Sure. Matt's been driving them since he was ten. Don't tell Mum though."

And off he went. But it didn't matter because Jenny had come.

We went out for a walk. "I'll show you the sights of Brilby," I said grandly. "Look, a house... another house... a river... a church... a house... a tree! Wow!"

Suddenly Jenny clutched my arm. "Oh yes," I said in a loud voice. "That's another of the sights of Brilby. Deadly Emily!"

I knew Emily heard me, because she sort of flinched. For a second I thought she was going to turn and go back the way she'd come. She was scared!

"Strange, isn't it? She doesn't act all big and tough when she hasn't got her gang with her."

"What's she doing here?" Jenny muttered.

"She lives here, unfortunately." I said it loudly on purpose. I wanted to see if Emily would say anything back.

She didn't. She looked right through us, pretending we weren't there, even though she had to step off the pavement to avoid us.

As she went past, I did something I'd never have dared to do at school. I grabbed the hood of her jacket. It was only fixed on with poppers, and it came off when I tugged it.

Emily spun round, "Give that back!"

I backed away, still holding it.

"Give it back, I said!"

"Say please, then."

She tried to grab it, but I threw it over her head. Jenny, looking terrified, managed to catch it. We threw the hood back and forth several times, with Emily as "pig in the middle". She looked ready to explode with fury.

Into my mind crept a feeling that I shouldn't be doing this, but I pushed the thought away. I was enjoying myself.

"Give it! Or else!" Emily yelled.

I said, "Ha! She can dish it out but she can't take it! I'm only doing the same as what you did to me last week, Emily. Remember? When my bag ended up in a puddle?"

There were several puddles to choose from. (There are always puddles in Brilby.) I found a nice muddy one, held the hood over it, and dropped it gently in.

"Oh dear, how careless of me."

"I'll get you," she hissed. "I'll get you for this."

"Oooh! I'm so frightened!"

We watched as she fished the hood out of the mud. It looked as if the fur lining would never be the same again, and I felt a tiny bit sorry.

"My dad's going to kill me," she said under her breath.

"Good. I hope he does," said Jenny recklessly. "Good riddance!"

"Now you know what it feels like – being bullied," I said to Emily. "Not nice, is it?"

She didn't answer, just walked away. I felt – I can't explain how I felt – sort of burning hot, powerful, triumphant! I also felt rather sick.

Now I knew what it felt like to be a bully.

CHAPTER 6

WORKS OF ART

The feeling of triumph didn't last for very long. I knew there would be trouble when Emily got back with her gang.

It didn't help when a letter arrived for Mum, telling her she'd got a job in an office in Caston. She jumped up and began to do a kind of dance - not easy in Gran's cluttered kitchen.

"Well done, lass," said Gran. "I told you it'd all come right in the end. We ought to celebrate - put kettle on, Emily. Emily! What's up? You look like you've lost a pound and found a sixpence."

For Mum's sake I tried to look pleased. I felt about as joyful as a prisoner in court, hearing the judge say, "Guilty! Life imprisonment!" Imprisonment in Brilby. Imprisonment in Caston School...

I said so to Tom as we sat on the bus, expecting him to feel the same.

"Oh come on," he said. "It isn't that bad."

I stared at him. "You mean you don't mind living here?"

"It's OK."

"But you hated it when we came!"

"Well, yeah. I didn't know anybody then, but I do now, and I'm in the football team and the rock climbing club. I could get to like it here. And so could you, if you'd give it a try."

"I don't like football, or rock climbing. I want to go back home!"

"You want to grow up a bit; that's what you want."

It wasn't fair. Nobody was on my side – not even Tom. If things got much worse I would... I would run away from home.

***

I called Denise, my best friend in London, and told her how awful things were. I even told her about all my prayers that weren't being answered. I knew Denise would understand. She was the one who took me along to St Mark's and helped me become a Christian.

She said, "We were talking about that, just this Sunday."

"Talking about me?"

"No, you idiot. About why God doesn't always give us what we ask for."

"Not always? It's never," I said bitterly. "Listen, I've been praying for ages about Mum and Dad, and about school, and Deadly Emily. But it doesn't make any difference. God must have stopped listening to me."

"I don't think God ever stops listening," she said cautiously, "or caring about us. But that doesn't mean he always gives us whatever we want."

"Why not?"

"It's like when I was little, I kept on and on at my dad. I wanted to go down the big slide in the playground. He always said no. But that didn't mean he hated me, did it? It meant the opposite."

"Yes, well... that was different. You were asking for something that might be bad for you."

"But at the time I didn't understand that. I was too little – I just thought he was being horrible."

"You mean when I get older and wiser," I said, "I'll understand that there was a good reason why my prayers weren't answered? Is that right?"

"Got it in one."

I thought about this. "But your dad didn't always say no. He did let you go on the slide in the end."

"Yeah – but only when he knew the time was right. So don't stop praying, OK?"

After the phone call I felt a whole lot better, and I realised how much I was missing the St Mark's Mob. In Brilby I had nobody to talk to – not about things that mattered. The church in Brilby was hopeless, unless you were fond of funerals: a bored vicar, a few old ladies in hats, no music because the organ had died years ago. I went twice; then I gave up.

Oh, I wished I could go back a year, to the time when I first believed in Jesus and gave my life to him. I felt so happy then. I felt as if all my troubles were over. Why did nobody warn me?

***

At least there was one bit of good news. Mrs Bell was off with the flu.

We had a new teacher called Miss Atkinson. She seemed (for a teacher) quite nice. She was keen on Art, which is my favourite subject.

She told us to paint a winter scene. Most people immediately did snow, snowmen, sledges, snow, more snow. Boring! I thought of winter in Brilby and drew dark clouds, trees bending in the wind, rain lashing down. It was all painted in shades of grey.

Miss Atkinson held my picture up in front of the whole class. "Now this is really effective. Look at it – you can almost feel the wetness of the rain. Well done!"

I couldn't help looking pleased. It was the first time any of my work had been praised for ages and ages. I picked up my brush to add a few final raindrops.

"Want some more?"

Emily was holding a jar of dirty paint-water over my picture. Slowly she began to tilt it. I tried to grab it – but too late.

"Look at it! You can feel the wetness!" she giggled.

I stared at the ruined picture. Sludge-brown water ran off the table into my lap. At that moment, if I could have found a way to murder Emily, I'd have done it – no question. Stab her with a craft knife? Burn her to death in the kiln?

"You, girl! Stand up!"

At first I thought it was me she was yelling at. But no – she meant Emily.

"It was an accident, Miss..."

"It was not an accident. I saw exactly what you did. You will apologise and clean up the mess, and you will spend every break time this week scrubbing paint pots!"

"Sorry," Emily mumbled. She glared at me.

I managed not to laugh out loud. If Mrs Bell had been in charge, Emily would have got away scot-free: "An accident? Oh dear. Be more careful next time. Denise, clear it up!"

Maybe Mrs Bell would develop pneumonia, pleurisy or pig fever. The longer she was away from school the better.

***

A few days later Miss Atkinson told us about an art competition. It was to design a poster that would make people want to visit your home town. I thought of a collage in the shape of Big Ben, using pictures of famous London sights. Dad could send me postcards and things.

When I sketched out my design, Miss Atkinson looked doubtful. "London? But this is a local competition. I think they're expecting posters about places near here."

"You said it was to be about our home town," I argued. "This isn't my home town. London is."

Miss Atkinson looked at the competition rules. "Well, there's nothing to say it has to be a local place. It just says 'your home town', but the competition is for schools within the county. You'd have a better chance of winning if you use the place you live in now."

I spent some time thinking. "It's no good; I can't do an advert for Brilby. There's nothing to advertise. VISIT BRILBY - IT'S BRILL! and a picture of nothing. Amazing!"

"Oh thanks, Denise," said Emily. "You just gave me an idea."

"You must be pretty desperate," I said.

"I suppose even a moron can have one good idea in a lifetime."

"Possibly," I said. "Do let us know when it arrives."

CHAPTER 7

THE OLD HOUSE

Mrs Bell was off sick right up to the Easter Holidays. Magic!

Even better, we were going to London for the Easter weekend to see Dad. I'd been looking forward to this for ages. We went on a coach – just Tom and me. Mum waved us off; Dad met us at the other end.

He wasn't alone, I was sorry to see. Paula, his girlfriend, was with him, waving and smiling as if it was her we'd come to see. She's one of those people who try so hard to be nice all the time that you can't tell what they're really like.

"Lovely to see you, Emily, Tom – I'm so glad you could come!" See – she was at it again. She tried to kiss me, but I fended her off.

Dad and Paula had a flat in Fulham. It was miles from Streatham, where we used to live. And it was completely unlike our old house. It was more like a hotel room before the guests arrive: not a cushion out of place; not one dirty cup in the sink. (How had Paula managed to tidy Dad up? Mum had often tried and failed.)

We were in London all right, but we hadn't come home. I felt a great ache of longing for my home – my real home: 12 Dorset Avenue, SW16. But it was sold, and someone else was living in it now. Someone else was sleeping in my bedroom... Whoever they were, I wished them bad dreams.

Although the homesick feeling refused to go away, I tried not to show it, because Dad was doing his best to give us a good time. We saw a film, we went to the zoo, and we had meals out (probably so we didn't mess up Paula's shiny kitchen). On the Saturday, Dad had got tickets for some football game Tom was desperate to see.

"What about me?" I said.

"I thought you might like to see your old friend, Denise," said Dad. "It's all arranged. Paula's going to take you over there and pick you up after tea."

Paula gave me a big smile and said she was looking forward to it, although you could bet Streatham was not her idea of an afternoon out. On the way there she kept trying to be bright and chatty. I gave her one-word answers and stared out of the window.

The High Road was busy, like it always is on a Saturday – crowded, noisy, alive. Compared to this,

Caston was only half-awake and Brilby was deep in a coma.

"Do you think... could we just have a look at my old house?" I said. "It's sort of on the way to Denise's place."

"Of course, we can. We're in plenty of time, sweetheart."

I guided her through the familiar streets. There was the pizza place, there was Gita's dad's shop, there was my school. I felt as if I was getting closer to the centre of a maze.

And there it was: number 12, Dorset Avenue. It hadn't changed a bit. There were even the same curtains at the windows, and the same weeds in the small front garden. It looked as if I could walk in and be home again. But I couldn't.

For a while I just gazed at the house. I had reached the centre of the maze – and there was nothing there, only emptiness.

"Poor darling," said Paula. "Do you miss it very much?"

I shook her hand off my shoulder. "I just wanted to see it, that's all. Who lives there now?"

"I don't know that anybody lives there. The man who bought it works in Saudi Arabia most of the time, your dad said."

Somehow that made it even worse – my house being empty, cold and unloved, my garden overgrown. (Mind you, that was nothing new. Dad loves gardening like the Queen loves bungee jumping.) Number 12 was not a home any more, just a building.

I shivered and said, "Come on, let's go."

***

At least Denise was still Denise. After the first two minutes, it felt as if I'd never been away. As if I was back to my real self again.

Of course Denise knew all about my name being taken away from me. "Nah, you don't look like a Denise," she said. "Not pretty enough. You're definitely still an Emily."

"Emilys," I said haughtily, "have got brains. We don't have to get by on our looks. We are intellectual... if you know what that means."

"Even Deadly Emily?"

"Oh, *she* doesn't count. She's really an Edna in disguise." At that moment Emily seemed small and harmless and very far away. "I wish you were living in Brilby, Denise. The two of us could soon sort Emily out."

"No way am I moving to Brilby," she said. "But I want to show you something. I read it this morning and I thought, Emily's got to see this."

41

She got her Bible from the shelf, and I thought guiltily of my own one, gathering fluff under the bed. I hadn't opened it for a while. It seemed like too much effort.

She showed me a bit she'd underlined in pencil: "Love your enemies, do good to those who hate you."

The words seemed to jump off the page and hit me right between the eyes: "Love your enemies."

"This must be a misprint," I said. "It can't mean that."

"Well, it says the same thing again further down." She pointed. "Love your enemies, do good to them..."

I said, "But nobody could love Deadly Emily. Even her so-called friends don't like her much – they only go round with her because they're scared not to. I bet her own mother doesn't love her."

"Maybe that's why she's the way she is. Deep down, she knows nobody likes her."

"Look, nobody likes *me* much at school, but that hasn't turned me into the Monster from Planet X, has it?"

"Hope not. Mum won't like it if you leave trails of slime all over my room."

I looked again at the words in the Bible. Jesus said them to his followers – I wondered if they were shocked by what he said.

But I was one of his followers too. So I couldn't just ignore what he said, could I? Even if it seemed difficult? (Correction, even if it seemed impossible.)

"Fine. OK. Love your enemies," I said. "Doesn't tell us how to do it, though."

"Well, it gives us a hint. Read on a bit – there."

"Do to others as you would have them do to you," I read. What did that mean? What it didn't mean was bullying Emily when I got the chance. Or making nasty comments. Or hating her so much that I almost enjoyed the hate...

"Not easy," said Denise. "But I'm going to give it a try."

"What? I didn't know you had any enemies."

She made a face. "Only my kid sister. She's always stirring up trouble and then telling Mum I started it. And I suppose there's Tanya at school – remember her? She's got worse since you left."

"I bet she's not as bad as Emily."

"No. She only gets five out of ten for horribleness. Emily sounds like an eight or even a nine."

"Denise!" I put on a shocked voice. "We shouldn't be talking about our enemies like this. We should be saying how nice and wonderful and attractive and loveable they are."

She giggled. "So are you going to give it a try, then? Loving Emily and doing good to her?"

"I might," I said. "I'll let you know."

CHAPTER 8

THE NEW HOUSE

When Mum met us from the coach at Caston, there was a big smile all over her face.

"Guess what. I think I've found us a house!"

"Oh, magic! Where is it? What's it like?"

"Wait and see."

We rattled back to Brilby on the bus, pestering Mum with questions. It was a bit like that game where you're only allowed to answer Yes or No.

"How big a house?"

"Wait and see."

"Is there a garden?"

"Wait and see."

"Will we have a bedroom each?"

'Wait and see. We'll have a look round it after tea."

"Oh," I said, disappointed. "It's in Brilby, then?"

"Yes," said Mum, caught off guard for a moment.

"But Mum! Why Brilby?" I cried. "Caston would be better. At least there's things to do in Caston..."

"I've thought about this a lot. If we stay in Brilby we'll be near Gran. She can be there when you come home from school, Emily. You know I don't get back till half-past five – and I don't like the thought of you going home to an empty house. And Gran can make your tea if I get held up at work."

"Yuk, I hate Gran's cooking – pale grey mince and lumpy custard."

"Both on the same plate?" said Tom.

"Oh, shut up. It's all right for you, you don't mind living in Brilby. You're turning into a local yokel, you know that? You even talk like one sometimes."

"Now then, now then," said Mum. "As I was saying when I was so rudely interrupted, there's another big advantage to Brilby."

"Oh sure. What is it? As much rain as you can drink?"

"No. Cheap houses. If we buy this one, we might have enough left over to get a car as well. Now don't get too excited, Tom, it wouldn't be a Ferrari. Something small and second-hand. But at least it would get us about the place."

"If we lived in Caston we wouldn't need a car," I muttered.

Mum sighed. "Oh, Emily. Give it a rest, will you? At least until you've seen the place."

After tea we set out to inspect the house. Gran lives at the top end of Brilby, which is really just one long narrow street. We were heading for the bottom end – and my heart sank deeper, the lower we went. Deadly Emily lived somewhere down there.

All the houses in Brilby look much the same – grey stone walls, grey slate roofs. The endless rain has washed away any colours they once had. But strangely enough it wasn't raining that evening. Over the moor was a blazing sunset which I suddenly wanted to paint.

We were almost out of the village when Mum stopped and knocked on a door. A smiling old lady opened it. (Brilby is full of old people – young ones escape as soon as they can.)

She showed us round the house, and I had to admit it wasn't bad. Two rooms downstairs, plus a decent kitchen. And three bedrooms, so Tom and I could have a proper bedroom each. It all looked OK, except that there were dogs everywhere – china ones, that is. They were even in the toilet.

"Aren't they lovely?" said the old lady. "They've been company for me since Fred died. Would you like to see the garden?"

The garden was nice – long and narrow, with the river running past at the bottom. The old lady said it was all too much for her since Fred died. She was moving to a flat in Caston.

"Are you taking all the china dogs?" I said.

"Oh yes," she said, shocked. "I'll find room for them somehow. At least they don't need much in the way of exercise."

Just then I heard a sharp voice on the other side of the garden wall. "Emily! Come in! Your tea's getting cold."

There was the sound of running feet, and a back door slammed. Tom and I looked at each other.

"What are the people next door like?" I asked.

"Oh, they're a funny lot. Keep themselves to themselves. I don't see much of them – never have done." She leaned forward and whispered something to Mum, but her whisper was loud enough to hear: "I think he drinks."

I said, "Is their name Smith? Is their daughter called Emily?"

"Yes, love. Do you know her?"

I tried to catch Mum's eye, but she started on a long discussion about curtains and carpets. I couldn't get a word in edgeways. At last we were out of the place and walking back up the hill.

"Well? What did you think?"

"Mum! We can't live there! It's right next door to Deadly Emily!"

"Yes," said Mum calmly. "So?"

"But Mum!"

"I don't see what's so terrible about living next door to her. You needn't see any more of her than you do at the moment, need you?"

"How do you know? You have no idea what she's like! She'll probably spy on me in the garden. She'll see all my things when we're moving in – and then laugh about them at school. I'm not living there! Never!"

"And what do you think, Tom?" said Mum.

"Er... it's very near the river," said Tom in a cautious kind of way. "Don't you get rising damp and wet rot and stuff?"

I gave him a grateful look, but Mum said, "Of course, I'll have the place checked over, just in case. At the moment it looks like very good value for money."

"Money! That's all you ever think about!"

"Emily, you know that's not true. I'm trying to do what's best for all of us. And I know we won't find another house at that price – not unless it's one that needs loads of work done on it. Do you want to go on living at Gran's for ever and ever?"

"No. But I'd rather live at Gran's than next door to Emily."

"Who knows? She might be a bit more friendly if we are neighbours."

"Oh yeah... and pigs might fly to Australia, non-stop, both ways."

CHAPTER 9

VILLAGE TALK

I hate the way grown-ups pretend to give you a choice, when really they've already decided for you. Like when Dad and Mum split up, they asked Tom and me who we wanted to live with – but they had already decided it would be Mum.

It was just the same with the house. Mum had made up her mind to buy it before we even saw it. So why bother to ask us if we liked it? We were going there, like it or not.

At least it wouldn't happen straight away. "These things take time," said Gran. "Be patient, young Emily. Buying a house is not like buying a bag of liquorice allsorts."

"I hope it takes years," I said, "Centuries... millenniums."

Mum just laughed. She was in a better mood these days. She liked her new job. She had stopped looking worried all the time. "It's because things are getting more settled," she said. One day she came home with her hair much shorter and quite a different colour.

Gran said, "What's all this in aid of? You look like mutton dressed as lamb."

"I think it looks great, Mum - suits you." I glared at Gran, who took no notice.

"I suppose you're going to start gadding about now, with this money you're earning. Out every night, and expecting me to babysit, I'll bet."

"Oh no," Mum said coolly. "If I do go out, Tom's quite old enough to take care of himself and Emily. And as for gadding about, I'm 38 you know, not 88. My life's not over yet!"

Oh help! What was that supposed to mean?

***

We were back at school. It was as awful as ever.

"Dear me," said Mrs Bell, looking at our books. "You don't seem to have done much while I was ill, do you?"

"No, Mrs Bell," said Emily, boot-licking as usual. "Miss Atkinson made us do Art nearly every day."

"Did she, indeed? In that case, we'll give Art a miss for the next few weeks. We've got some catching up to do."

Everyone turned and scowled at Emily. She didn't look too pleased herself. Although I hated to admit it, she wasn't at all bad at Art, and Miss Atkinson had liked her entry for the poster competition. It showed Brilby with the stream in the foreground. The stream looked wider than in real life, the houses were prettier and the moors more purple; plus there wasn't a cloud in the sky. Apart from that it was quite realistic.

My collage of London was pretty good too. Dad had sent me heaps of material, enough for about six posters – photos, theatre tickets, even guidebooks. When I rang to thank him he said, "Actually, it's Paula you should be thanking. She collected most of it."

"Oh, right! Say thanks for me, will you?"

Too late... Paula was on the line, burbling on about how wonderful she knew my picture must be, and asking what the prize was.

"Railway tickets worth two hundred pounds," I said. "You can choose where to go."

"Oh, super! When you win you must come and see us."

Sure, sure.

Later on I thought about what she'd said. Two hundred pounds would be more than enough to get me to London – wouldn't it? But not to go and visit Paula! That was not what I had in mind.

***

In a village, news soon gets around. It wasn't long before Emily found out we would be moving in next door to her. Big trouble!

I was waiting at the bus stop after school. This was the time of day I really dreaded. Until Tom got onto the bus, two stops later, I was all alone with the gang.

On a good day, the bus would arrive straight away; on a bad day, it wouldn't. On a good day, the gang would ignore me completely; on a bad day...

"Hey, Dense! Is it true what my mum says, that you're trying to move in next door?"

They all crowded round me, pushing, shoving, breathing into my face. My insides felt as if they were dropping down in a lift. Stay cool – stay cool. Don't let them see they're getting to you...

"Dense! I asked you a question. Don't you know it's rude not to answer?"

"Maybe she's deaf as well as dumb," giggled Rosie.

"Why don't you mind your own business?" I said to Emily.

"But it is my business. Riff-raff from London moving in next door! We don't want you, understand?"

"Strangely enough," I said, "I'm not exactly longing to move in next to you."

"Then don't. Just go back where you came from."

"Yeah, we don't want you here. You stink."

"When did you last have a bath, Dense?"

"You've got nits. Look, there's one!" Rachel pulled my hair, and I took a step backwards. But they moved in closer, like hyenas round a lump of meat.

Oh, why wouldn't the bus come? I looked over my shoulder. It was nowhere in sight.

"Why did she come here in the first place?"

"Cos her dad ran off with his fancy woman."

"Don't blame him, do you? Not if Dense's mum is anything like Dense."

How did they know about Dad? Had Jenny told them? No... more likely Gran had talked to her friends, and now the whole of Brilby knew.

"Her mum was on the bus this morning," said Emily. "She's the one with dyed hair and a skirt three sizes too tight. You must have seen her."

"Oh yes. The one who sat next to poor little Dense in case poor little Dense felt lonely on the bus."

"Holding her hand... changing her nappy..."

Suddenly I remembered another bit of Brilby gossip. Gran had mentioned it when she heard who our new neighbours were going to be: "Just to warn you, like... although it may not be true. I'm only going by what folk said at the time..."

I said, "Talking of families, what about yours, Emily? It sounds quite exciting. Didn't your dad get blind drunk once, and throw your mum down the stairs?"

"What did you say?" Two bright pink spots appeared on Emily's cheeks.

"I said, your dad got blind drunk and threw your mum down the stairs. She broke her arm. Then she told people it was an accident because she was scared of what he'd do. Isn't that right?"

"Who told you that?" said Emily in a voice so quiet it was dangerous.

"Oh, everybody knows," I said cheerfully. "It's all around Brilby."

"Well it's NOT TRUE! It's a LOAD OF RUBBISH!"

Emily hit me in the face – very hard. I stumbled backwards and fell off the kerb.

There was a horrible high squealing noise and a lot of shouting. I opened my eyes. Right next to my face was something huge and black – after a while I realised it was the wheel of a bus.

"Are you all right, love? Can you sit up?"

The bus driver was kneeling beside me, his face as grey as the pavement. I moved my arms and legs a bit. Everything still seemed to be attached. Slowly and carefully I sat up, trembling like a very old lady. And then I fainted.

CHAPTER 10

A LOT OF FUSS

You would not believe the amount of fuss that was made. A trip to hospital for me (I woke up in the ambulance), and a bad fright for Mum, when a garbled message reached her at work. She thought I had actually been run over. She ordered a taxi and rushed to the hospital, where I was sitting with my feet up watching "Neighbours".

The bus company sent a letter to the school, saying children at bus stops should be kept under control. They also pointed out that if the bus driver hadn't reacted so quickly, "a fatality might have resulted". In other words, my story would have ended right here.

The head teacher, Miss Green, read the letter to the whole school. "And I want to see Denise, Emily, Rose, Rachel and Charlotte in my office, straight after assembly."

She gave us a long lecture. Then she took us outside and made us look at the skid marks in the road. Two long black snakes, ending just where my head had been lying... I felt a bit sick.

"Denise, come back to my office please. The rest of you can go to your classroom – for now."

Oh, help! Now what? Even more trouble?

She sat me down and said quite kindly, "Now, Denise, I know you haven't had an easy time since you joined this school. I know you and Emily don't exactly get on."

She paused and looked at me expectantly. I said nothing.

"I'd like you to tell me what happened that afternoon at the bus stop."

Suddenly I realised that this was my chance to drop Emily right in it. *She pushed me, miss, she pushed me right in front of the bus. She wanted to kill me...*

Somehow I couldn't say it. After all it wasn't true, was it? She had hit me, but she hadn't pushed me off the pavement. And she wouldn't have hit me if I hadn't said those things about her dad.

And then I remembered something: *Love your enemies and do good to those who hate you.*

I had forgotten all about it. At the bus stop, when Emily said things that hurt me, all I thought of was getting back at her. Why hadn't I kept my big mouth shut? I could have said nothing at all – like Jesus did when people mocked him and hurt him.

"Well?" said Miss Green. "Don't be afraid. Just tell me what happened."

I swallowed hard. "We had an argument. She said some things; I said some things. She hit me, and I stepped back and then I fell off the kerb. It was an accident, really..."

"Are you sure?"

I nodded.

"The reason I'm asking is because a man who was passing said that one of the girls pushed you over – actually pushed you in front of the bus."

"No, Miss Green. It wasn't like that."

"All right. But next time someone starts any trouble, you must come and tell me at once. Remember that."

Suddenly I imagined her as Superman, swooping down to the rescue, glasses gleaming and cardigan flying. "Is it a bird? Is it a plane? No! It's SUPER-HEAD! Pow! Zap!"

"Thank you, Denise, you can go now. Ask Mrs Bell to send Emily here, will you please?"

***

I never did find out what Miss Green said to Emily, but it must have been pretty bad. She kept out of my way for ages.

Eventually all the fuss died down. My bruises faded and so did the skid marks in the road. Nothing was left...

except the memory of Emily's face just before she hit me. What I said had really got to her, hadn't it?

"It's not true! It's a load of rubbish!"

In that case, Emily, why get so upset?

CHAPTER 11

A NOISE IN THE NIGHT

It was moving day. A furniture van arrived bringing beds and sofas and things that had been in storage since the London house was sold. In the new house they looked odd, sort of ill at ease. None of them matched with the carpets.

"Never mind," said Mum briskly. "They'll have to do for now."

The next job was to shift all our other stuff down the hill from Gran's house. Matthew Preston's dad let us borrow an ancient Land Rover, which was a big help. Otherwise we would have been walking up and down that hill for weeks.

We unpacked boxes and found things we hadn't seen for ages: all my books and DVDs, my doll's house (I'm too old for it, but I keep it because Dad built it for me), our bikes, Mum's sewing machine and Tom's computer games (which he played for the next three days solid).

Although I hadn't wanted to move, at least not into this house, I liked it once we were actually in. It was fantastic to have my own room again, and my own bed. I spent ages arranging all my things, then rearranging them. There was a big cupboard, built into the thickness of the wall, which swallowed up most of my odds and ends.

"I wonder which bedroom Deadly Emily has," I said. The house next door was joined on to ours; it looked exactly the same but the opposite way round. Their front door was on the right, ours was on the left. If Emily's bedroom was above the back door, like mine, then our two rooms would be side by side.

"What are you worried about?" asked Tom. "That her X-ray eyes will see you through the wall?"

"She might hear things."

"Oh, talk to yourself in there, do you? First sign of madness!"

Mum said, "These old houses were built with good thick walls. I don't think you could hear a brass band through them. Have you heard any noise from her side?"

"No."

"Well then."

"What's so funny?" I said to Tom.

"Oh nothing... just thinking about you and Emily listening for each other." He leaned his ear to the wall. "Shhh! Don't move! No, can't hear anything." He turned and listened the other way. "Shhh! Don't move! No, can't hear anything... You might be *this* close to her all the time."

"Oh, shut up."

Tom said idly, "How old is this house, anyway? Do we know?"

"1852, it said in the deeds," Mum told him. "This whole row was built then for the mine workers and their families."

"Mine? What mine?"

"The old copper mines further up the valley," said Mum. "They were shut down years ago, before I was born. There was a big accident - people got killed. Ask Gran about it if you're interested."

"Didn't we see the place once, ages and ages ago?" said Tom. "We were out on a walk with you and Dad. I wanted to go in and explore, but you wouldn't let me."

"That's right," said Mum. "They're dangerous."

I vaguely remembered the place. "They didn't look like mines though, more like caves - holes in the hill."

Mum said, "I mean it now. They're dangerous - don't go near them."

***

On Thursdays Tom had karate lessons after school, so Gran came down to our house until Mum got home from work. If Mum was going to be late Gran would usually start to cook the supper. This gave her the chance to snoop around our kitchen, saying things like, "Don't you keep any suet in this house? And what's this lasaggny stuff – are you meant to eat it?"

To distract her from this, I asked her about the old copper mines. I was interested – I don't know why – maybe because men who worked there had lived in our house, long ago.

"Oh, aye, I remember the old mines. They were still being worked when I were a lass, right up till the big accident, and that finished them. Mind you, people did say they would have shut down anyway – copper was all but gone."

"What was the accident?" I said.

"Roof fell in. Seven men were trapped, and only two of them came out alive. My Uncle Josh was one – your great-great-uncle. He got out, but he left his foot behind!"

"What?"

"Well, they had to cut his foot off to get him out of the mine. It was trapped, like. After that he had a metal leg with a shiny black shoe on it – I remember it well. He used to say he had one foot in the grave already."

"And what about the others – the ones that died?"

"Aye, five of them, all Brilby men. They're buried in churchyard. Brilby was never the same after that. The mine shut down, and folk had to leave to get work where they could... No, it was never the same."

I shivered. There was a question I wanted to ask, but I didn't because I was scared of the answer.

The men who died – had any of them lived in this house?

***

I woke up suddenly in the night. My luminous clock said 1:18. In the silence of the house, I thought I could hear a sound... someone crying.

It must be Mum. What was the matter? Had she heard some bad news, something too awful to tell us?

I crept out of bed and onto the landing, but as I did, the sound faded. When I went back into my own room, I could hear it again. Not very loud – the sort of noise you make when no one must hear you crying, but you just can't help it – sobbing and sobbing, lost, lonely, afraid.

This sound was in the room with me. I could feel my skin prickle all over.

I groped my way into Mum's room and whispered her name.

"What is it?" she said groggily.

"I'm scared, Mum. There's a noise in my room."

"What on earth are you on about?"

She heaved herself out of bed, went into my bedroom and switched the light on. "What noise? I can't hear any noise."

I listened... Silence, apart from the patter of rain on the roof.

"It went away when you put the light on," I said.

"Oh, Emily. You must have had a bad dream. Get back to bed, it's school in the morning." She yawned.

"Can I sleep in your bed, Mum? Please..."

"I suppose so. Come on, then."

She went to sleep at once, but I didn't. I was listening for the noise.

Had I heard the ghost of someone who'd lived here long ago? A woman whose husband had died in the mine? A child who couldn't understand why Dad had left one morning and never come home? A voice without hope, sobbing and sobbing... It seemed like years before I got to sleep.

CHAPTER 12

GHOST STORIES

In the morning it all seemed a bit silly. Tom was interested, though. He looked around my room and asked where the sound had seemed to come from.

"I don't know," I said. "It felt like it was here, in the room. When I went out of the door it got fainter."

"Sure it wasn't the wind blowing in the chimney? That sounds dead spooky sometimes."

"There wasn't any wind last night. Anyway, that makes a howling noise. This was more like... sort of sobbing."

"A child or a grown-up?"

"Don't know."

"Well, next time you hear it, don't wake Mum up – wake me, Tom Smith, Ghostbuster. If there's a ghost here I want to see it too."

"I hope it never comes back," I said. "Never."

I didn't want to go to bed that night. My bedroom that I had liked so much seemed threatening now. The open cupboard was like a black gaping mouth. I shut it quickly.

Mum said I could go to sleep with the light on, just this once.

But it was all right. There were no more noises, or if there were, they didn't wake me up.

It was weeks since Emily had given me any trouble. Ever since the bus incident, she had kept out of my way and I'd kept out of hers. We had been moved to different tables at school, which helped.

Even after we moved in next door, I hadn't seen much of her. Or any of her family, either. "They keep themselves to themselves" – that was true all right. A high wall surrounded their garden. Their windows had net curtains top to bottom.

Emily's mum didn't seem to go out much. When she did, she would scurry along keeping close to the wall, like a mouse afraid of being seen.

"And she never says hello, not to a soul," said Gran. "Just gives a little nod, like, and goes past."

Mum laughed. "That would be quite normal behaviour in London."

"Aye, but this isn't London, is it? In Brilby, folk think she's stand-offish."

"Is it really true her husband got drunk and threw her down the stairs?" I said. "He doesn't look the type, somehow." He was a small, grey-looking man who worked at an office in Caston.

"It's the quiet ones you want to watch out for," Gran said darkly.

Mum said, "Don't believe all you hear, Emily. Stories like that get added to every time people tell them. Probably she tripped over his shoe or something, and fell downstairs..."

"Well, I don't know," said Gran. "No smoke without fire, is what I always say. She was wearing dark glasses the other day and it wasn't even sunny out. Now why would that be? I bet she was covering up a big black eye."

"Oh dear," said Mum. "Remind me never to wear sunglasses in Brilby."

***

It was a Thursday, Tom's karate night, so I was alone when I got off the bus. Emily was alone too. None of her gang lived in Brilby. In fact no other girls lived in Brilby, unless you counted the Fawcett twins, aged 2.

What a waste, I thought suddenly. The only two girls in the village, and here we were ignoring each other, walking on opposite sides of the road. If Emily were a different person, living in Brilby would be much more fun. It would be great to have Denise, say, living next door – or even Jenny.

I thought back to how the war had begun: a quarrel over a seat in the bus – how stupid! If only I had a time machine, I'd go back in time and change those few moments...

All right, so I couldn't change the past. But could I change the future? I could try an experiment. I could try treating Emily as if she was a human being. (Do to others as you would have them do to you.)

"Hey, Emily!" I called, before I had time to chicken out. I half-expected her to ignore me. But she turned and looked in my direction.

Crossing to her side of the road, I said, "There's something I wanted to ask you." A wary look came onto her face. "Have you ever heard... has anyone ever said our house might be haunted?"

I could tell the question surprised her. She thought for a minute.

"No. I've never heard anything like that. Old Mrs Higgins lived there for years, and she never said a thing about ghosts."

I remembered the smiley old lady and her china dogs. She didn't look like someone who'd be interested in ghosts, unless they were four-legged ones.

"What makes you think it's haunted, then?" asked Emily.

"I heard a noise in the middle of the night. Nobody else heard it – they were asleep. Mum thinks it was just a bad dream, but it wasn't. I know it wasn't."

Emily looked nervously around her. "You do get noises in an old house," she said. "In my bedroom there's a creaky floorboard that my dad just can't fix - he's tried lots of times. It creaks now and then, even when nobody's walking about. When I was little I thought it was the bogeyman."

Excited, I said, "Maybe it's the ghost - the same ghost. They can walk through walls, can't they? I wonder if our bedrooms are next to each other."

"My one's over the kitchen."

"So's mine. They are next to each other!"

Both of us were silent for a moment.

"I wonder who the ghost is, if there is one," said Emily at last.

"Tom says the older a house is, the more people have died in it."

All at once she said, "Listen, you're not making this up, are you? Trying to scare me?"

"No, I'm not, honest."

"Well, tell me if you hear any more noises. And I'll tell you if I do."

I was surprised to see that we were outside my house. We had walked all the way down the hill like two ordinary people - not like enemies at all.

"Tata then," said Emily.

"Bye."

I went in. Gran was knitting in front of our TV.

"Gran, you'll never believe this. I just walked home with Deadly Emily! And I'm still alive to tell the tale!"

But all Gran's attention was on Postman Pat. "That's nice, love," she said. "Put kettle on, will you?"

CHAPTER 13

WINNERS AND LOSERS

Things changed after that – but only slightly. If I was with Tom or Jenny, I never spoke to Emily. And she ignored me when her gang was around.

Just occasionally, if we happened to meet, we might talk – almost secretly, like two spies swapping passwords.

"How's the ghost?"

"Keeping very quiet – maybe it's gone on holiday."

"I heard the floorboard creak again last night."

Once I tried tapping on the bedroom wall, but she didn't reply. Perhaps she wasn't there, or perhaps, as Mum had said, the walls were too thick to let sounds travel through.

***

One day in assembly Miss Green said she had a special announcement to make.

"Many of you entered an art competition last term. There were several very good entries and I'm pleased to tell you one of them has won a prize! Here's Mr Jackson from the Tourist Board, who is going to present it."

A smart-looking man stepped onto the platform with a white envelope in his hand. It was like one of those TV award shows, where everyone tells everyone else how wonderful they are.

"The first prize winner in the Junior School section is: Emily Smith!"

All Emily's friends began to clap, and Mrs Bell gave her a huge beaming smile like a toothpaste advert.

"Come out to the front, Emily, please."

Oh well. I didn't mind too much – not nearly as much as I would have done a few weeks before. It would have been nice, though...

The man shook hands with Emily and gave her the envelope. "No, don't go just yet, Emily. I wanted to tell you what the judges thought of your entry. They liked it so much that even though London isn't exactly a local tourist attraction, they still felt it deserved to win."

London? Wait a minute! He was talking about my poster! I put my hand up, but nobody noticed.

"The collage of Big Ben was very striking and effective..." I saw a look of doubt cross Emily's face.

"And the slogan tied in with it well. LONDON – FOR THE TIME OF YOUR LIFE."

I couldn't sit still any longer. I headed for the front of the hall. "Denise! Sit down at once!" hissed Mrs Bell, but I ignored her.

"Excuse me," I said loudly. "I think you've got the wrong Emily Smith."

"I beg your pardon?"

"The poster of London – it was mine. *That* Emily's poster was all about Brilby." For a moment I thought Emily was going to deny it. I said quickly, "If you don't believe me you can ask Miss Atkinson."

"That won't be necessary," said Miss Green. "I'm sorry about the confusion, Mr Jackson. The fact is, we have two Emily Smiths in the school. We usually know this one by the name of Denise, and she is the Londoner – as I expect you can tell."

What did she mean by that? It didn't sound like a compliment... Anyway, who cared? I had won! First prize!

Emily, bright red in the face, got down from the platform, and I went up. In a kind of daze I stood there, clutching the prize, while Mr Jackson went through his little speech for the second time.

Back in the classroom I opened the white envelope. It held a posh-looking certificate and a travel voucher, both inscribed "Emily Smith". Everyone crowded round to have a look.

Just for a moment I caught sight of Emily. I didn't like the look on her face - not one little bit.

***

I could hardly wait to tell Tom when he got on the bus. After he had admired my prize I put it carefully in my coat pocket.

"So where are you taking us?" he said.

"Don't know. Maybe we could all go to the seaside. Or Mum said she'd like to visit York."

I didn't tell him my original plan - the one I'd made months ago, when things at school were so awful. Had I seriously thought of running away to London? Crazy...

We walked down the hill in the pouring rain. It didn't depress me - nothing could. Until, that is, I got home, hung up my coat, and looked in the pocket for my prize.

"Tom! The prize... it's gone!"

"What? Don't be daft. Are you sure you had it in that pocket?"

Frantically I checked all my pockets, my bag, my pockets again. "I know I put it in here... on the bus... remember?"

"Then there's only two places it can be. Still on the bus, or somewhere between here and the bus stop. Come on! I'll help you look."

"Or else somebody's nicked it," I said. "You know how people sort of brush past you as they're getting off the bus? I think Emily did that today. She could have slipped a hand into my pocket, easy as anything..."

"But why bother?" said Tom. "It's not like nicking money. The thing's made out in your name, so it's worthless to anyone else unless..."

"Exactly," I said. "Unless their name is Emily Smith."

CHAPTER 14

THINGS THAT GO BUMP IN THE NIGHT

When Mum got home we told her all about it. I wanted to go next door at once, bang on the door and demand my prize back. But she wouldn't let me.

"Emily, listen. You've got absolutely no proof she took it – none at all. Maybe it fell out of your pocket. Have you thought of that? The first thing we do is report it missing. Perhaps somebody found it and handed it in."

"And if not?"

"Then we'll write to the Tourist Board, or the railway. I don't know... they might cancel the ticket and send you another one, if they're feeling generous."

"What would happen then, if Emily used the stolen ticket? Would she get arrested?"

"Didn't I tell you, forget about Emily unless you get some kind of proof? Wild accusations are not proof. Just because you don't like someone doesn't mean they're a thief."

Tom said, "Don't worry, I bet you a quid it gets handed in by the end of the week."

I won the bet. It wasn't handed in.

I rang Denise and told her what had happened.

"I've had enough of this 'love your enemy' stuff. It's no use. Doesn't work."

"What d'you mean, doesn't work?"

"I thought if I was nice to her, she'd be nice to me. And she was, for a bit. Well, at least we were talking. But now see what she's done! The Bible was wrong!"

"Wait a minute, it didn't say..."

"I told you it must be a misprint, didn't I?"

"It didn't say, love your..."

"Well, I'm not going to bother any more. I'm going back to hating my enemies."

"Emily! Shut up just for one second, will you? Jesus didn't say love your enemies and then they'll love you."

"Didn't he?"

"Not when he already knew his own enemies were going to end up killing him. It wouldn't have made sense. Would it?"

"Oh, I thought..."

"Hold on. I want to check exactly what he did say."

I held on, hoping this wasn't going to use up all the credit on my mobile.

Denise picked up her phone again. "This is what it actually says: 'Love your enemies, do good to them... then your reward will be great, and you will be God's children'."

"It's still not right. Your reward will be great? What's so great about having my prize nicked off me?"

"Maybe it means in heaven. You'll get your reward in heaven."

"I don't know if I can wait that long," I said.

I felt angry and mixed-up inside. God seemed a long way away – if there was a God. Maybe there wasn't. Maybe all believers were just idiots.

***

"What do you think Mum meant by proof, exactly?" I asked Tom.

Mum had gone out for the evening. She had a date with a man! "Oh, he's nobody special, just someone from work," she'd said, but she still spent about two hours deciding what to wear.

It was quite cosy, just Tom and me, with a packet of chocolate digestives and a horror movie. Tom had borrowed the DVD from a friend at school. ("And if you tell Mum, I'll cut you up bit by bit, fry you and eat you.")

"Proof about what?" Tom said absently.

"Oh, you know... Emily stealing my prize."

He thought for a moment. "I suppose you'd need to find it in her possession – find where she hid it, that means."

"How do I do that? Break into her house?"

"Hmmm... difficult! But maybe it wouldn't be in her house, especially if she has the sort of mum that hoovers and dusts all the time."

"But that means it could be anywhere!"

"I've just remembered something," he said. "Ages ago, I was up the hill with Matt, getting some sheep in, and I saw her in the distance. You'll never guess where."

"In the graveyard? Digging up bodies?"

"Emily! This movie must be affecting your brain... No, she was going up the track that leads to the old mines. Matt thought it was odd at the time. There aren't any houses or farms or anything up that way."

"You mean she could have a secret den somewhere!"

"Yeah. That valley would be perfect. Nobody ever goes up there, except for the sheep."

"I'm going to follow her next time she goes out," I said. "Jenny's coming round on Saturday – she'll help."

Soon I got bored with the horror film and went up to bed. I lay awake for a while, making plans. I was just drifting off to sleep, when...

What was that? Someone screaming?

I sat up in bed. The sound had come from downstairs... Oh yes, of course, it must be Tom's DVD.

Then I heard a door slam – that sounded much nearer. At the same time, there was a movement in the corner of my room. The door of my cupboard slowly, gently swung open...

I sat frozen. My room was almost dark. The inside of the cupboard was blacker than the deepest black hole in outer space. What was in there? Was it coming out?

What came out, after a moment, was the voice of the ghost. It was like the last time – the heartbroken cry, the endless sobbing that would never be comforted – it went on and on, and I could not bear it... I could not bear it.

Mum, come back quick! Get rid of it like last time!

But no one came.

Oh God, help me – oh God, help me. Make it stop. Show me what to do.

After a minute I remembered Tom downstairs. Trembling, I got out of bed – this meant going past that awful door – and slipped silently down. I touched Tom's shoulder and he jumped about a mile in the air.

"Oh, it's you! What d'you go and do that for?"

"Tom... the ghost... it's come back!"

He sighed. "I knew I shouldn't let you watch this movie. You've been dreaming about it, haven't you?"

"No, it's really there. It's in my cupboard..."

"A haunted cupboard? That's new." He got up. "OK, let's see it."

When he reached my bedroom door he stopped suddenly, and I knew he had heard it. Then he went slowly into the room. I thought he was incredibly brave. From the doorway I watched him go right up to the cupboard and look in.

"There's nothing to see," he whispered, coming out of the room. "But you're right. It does sound like it's in the cupboard..."

"Put the light on," I begged.

"No, wait, I want to try something."

He went back in and I followed. I was sweating all over. Downstairs another horror victim was screaming, but scarier by far was the noise in my room. It was quieter now, like a child who's cried so much that no tears are left... Oh, stop! Please stop!

Tom went right into the cupboard, which was just about big enough to stand up in. He knocked on the wall at the back of it, quite loudly, three times. And at once the crying stopped.

We held our breath. There was a tiny scuffling sound, and then silence.

Tom beckoned me into his own room. He said quietly, "It isn't a ghost."

"W-what is it then?"

"I think it's somebody locked in a cupboard – another cupboard right next to yours, in Emily's house."

CHAPTER 15

INTO DARKNESS

I gaped at him. "Who is it, then? Is it Emily?"

"Seems likely, doesn't it? Or I suppose it could be her mum. Or maybe there's another child hidden away in there that nobody knows about. The Child in the Iron Mask!"

"Tom," I said. "This isn't funny."

"No, you're right. It isn't. I wouldn't like to be shut in that cupboard all on my own. There isn't even room to sit down."

"Why would they shut her in? She must have done something really awful." I thought of the things I knew about that Emily had done. Bad as they were, she didn't deserve such suffering, such hopeless, helpless weeping.

I went back to my room to listen. But everything was silent. Was she still there, imprisoned? Would she be there all night?

I didn't want to think about it. Gently I closed my cupboard door.

***

When Jenny came on Saturday, I told her all about my fright in the night. We looked in my cupboard, which seemed quite innocent by daylight.

"Tom thinks the wall must be quite thin between the two cupboards – that's why we could hear her. And when they slammed her door, the shock waves sort of travelled through and made my door move – wasn't half scary!"

"I bet," said Jenny. "Did you tell your mum?"

"Yes."

"What's she going to do?"

"Nothing," I said reluctantly. "She says it's none of our business and we shouldn't go stirring up trouble – not unless we know there's real, actual cruelty going on. But there is – she'd understand if she heard it for herself!"

"It sounded really bad, then?"

I nodded. "It was like... like the last person left alive after an earthquake or something. No family left, no friends, no home; just wanting to die..."

"That doesn't sound much like Emily," said Jenny doubtfully.

"No. Well, we don't know it was her. I wanted to see how she looked the next day, but she wasn't at school. And the day after that she seemed quite OK."

"Hold on a minute," said Jenny. "I did notice something. Yesterday, when we were getting changed after PE, she took off her T-shirt dead slow, like it was hurting her – and she had two great big bruises, one on each arm. Then she saw me looking and she goes, 'What are you staring at?' – so I didn't hang about."

"Bruises on *both* arms?"

"Yeah. You wouldn't get that if you just fell over, would you?"

"Not unless you were sumo wrestling at the time."

"It looked like somebody held her like this," (she grabbed me by the upper arms) "really tight like, and maybe shook her."

"All right, all right! No need to overdo it," I said dizzily.

Just then I heard a distant sound – the slam of a front door. Looking out of Mum's window, we saw Emily setting off up the road with a bag on her back.

"Where's she off to now?"

"I think I know. Come on – we'll follow her."

This was what I had planned to do, to look for my missing prize. But the prize now seemed a lot less important than solving the mystery of Emily Smith.

***

We went through the village slowly and cautiously, but Emily, a long way in front, didn't look round.

Further up the valley we lost sight of her because of the twists in the road. We turned onto the copper-mine track, and Jenny said, "How d'you know she came this way?"

"I don't. I'm guessing."

Each time we rounded a corner, I wondered if Emily would be in view. Each time the track was empty. Then suddenly, round yet another bend, the valley opened out. Here and there were heaps of stones which looked as if they had once been buildings. A battered sign said: "DANGER. KEEP OUT".

"Look. That's one of the mines over there."

It was like a small cave in the hillside. The opening was hardly as tall as a man, and it did not look man-made. Any minute, you felt, a big brown bear might come out of it, snarling.

"I bet she's here somewhere," I whispered. "I've got a strange feeling... like we're being watched."

Jenny looked round uneasily. "Weird kind of place. What would she want to come here for?"

I said, "If you want to get away from everybody, this is the place."

We wandered round the ruins. No sign of a den or hiding place. All we found were two more mine holes and a dead sheep.

"Can we go back now?" said Jenny. "I don't like it here."

"In a minute. I wonder where she went..."

All at once I thought I saw a movement in the corner of my eye. It was only for an instant – a pale flicker in the dark doorway of a mine. Or had I imagined it?

My mobile phone had quite a good light on it. When I aimed it into the mine entrance, we saw a narrow passage with rough rocky walls. Water went drip – drip – drip – onto the wet floor.

Was that a sound from deep in the tunnel? I listened, but it was now as dark and still as the depths of a well.

"Emily!" I called. A hollow echo of my voice came back. "Emily, it's me, Em – I mean Denise. Can I talk to you?" ...you? ...you?

No reply.

"It's about the ghost" ...ghost ...ghost.

"I'm sure she's in there," I said to Jenny.

"In there? I wouldn't go in for a million quid; I wouldn't. It's not safe."

I vaguely remembered my mum saying that too. But I hated the thought of going home again defeated, beaten by Emily.

Jenny said, "What's that? Shine the light over there a bit more."

Not far inside the tunnel was a little pile of stones, and leading out from it... what was that? I couldn't quite see. I took a couple of steps into the tunnel.

"Jenny! Look!" I whispered. "Someone's been in here, for certain."

She crept up alongside me. "Oh wow! A bit of string! Big deal."

"Don't you see? It's a way of finding your way back to the entrance, to make sure you don't get lost in the tunnels."

The string, held at one end by the heap of stones, snaked off into the darkness. Where did it lead? A secret cavern? A hidden treasure? Emily's den? But oh, it was so dark – and suppose the string broke!

"You're never going in there. You're daft as a brush," said Jenny.

That decided it. "Wait here," I said firmly. "I won't be long."

The first time I looked back I could still see the entrance, a small oval of light, but then the tunnel twisted, and it was gone. Now the only light was from my mobile. All around was darkness so thick you could almost touch it. And it was cold – a damp coldness like the inside of a fridge.

The roof was not far over my head, with all the weight of the hillside above it. What if it gave way? Was this where the accident happened all those years ago?

I nearly turned back then, but the string reassured me. It must be leading somewhere, surely. Still it went on into the darkness, past a couple of places where the tunnel branched in two.

Then came a place where it left the ground and travelled upwards, looping over outcrops of the rocky wall. I followed its path with the narrow beam of light, and kept on walking. Incredibly careless!

I never even saw the hole in the ground. I fell straight in like a deer into a trap.

CHAPTER 16

NOT ALONE

Dark... it was so dark...

I rubbed my eyes. They were open, but I couldn't see a thing. Had I gone blind? Where on earth was I?

I was lying on something stony, cold and hard. I was shivering, I couldn't see, and whenever I moved my ankle it felt as if somebody had stuck a knife in it.

Very slowly, memories came back to me, like bits of a dream when you wake. Looking for Emily... walking through the mine... falling...

"Help!" I shouted as loudly as I could. My voice echoed along the empty tunnels. Would Jenny ever hear me? How long before she realised something was wrong?

I put my hands out and felt rocky walls on either side. There was rock behind me too. In front I could feel nothing - not even a floor; I seemed to be on a narrow ledge.

Suddenly I remembered my phone. Where was it? I searched all around with my hands, but couldn't find it. I must have let go of it when I fell. It had vanished into the depths of the mine.

That was when I began to cry. I felt I would die there, alone in the dark.

Oh God, please help me, please. You said you would protect me. Why did you let me get into this mess?

Silence. I shouted until I was hoarse; then the silence pressed in again, and the darkness squeezed against my eyeballs.

Help me, God! Help me! Oh, why did you make this happen?

But that was stupid, blaming God. There was only one person to blame really – me! Mum had said to keep away from the mines. If only I'd done what she said!

Sorry, Mum, it won't happen again. I'm sorry, God – really sorry. Please forgive me. I know I've gone away from you, but I want to come back. Am I allowed to come back?

Then a strange thing happened. A kind of warmth and strength went right through me from head to toe. I stopped shivering; I stopped feeling scared.

And I knew God still loved me. Amazing! Even though I had made a total mess of things. Even there, alone in the dark, I was being held safe in the palm of his hand. So there was nothing to fear – not even if I was going to die. Living or dying, God still loved me; he would never leave me or forsake me.

I felt quite calm and peaceful. It was very strange.

And just then I noticed a slow lightening of the darkness. I began to see the pale shape of my own hand. The light grew; not torchlight but a flickering glow like a candle. I could make out the top of the hole, as high above me as a bedroom window. A face looked down.

"Denise, you are an idiot," said Emily. "Why can't you look where you're going?"

I never thought I could be so pleased to see Emily. For a moment I couldn't speak.

"Well?" she said. "Are you still alive?"

"Yes. But I've hurt my foot."

She moved the candle around the sides of the hole. "Looks like there was a ladder here once. But there's not much left of it – I don't think it's safe. We need a rope or something."

"Have you got one?"

"Even if I had, I can't get you out on my own, can I? I'll have to go and get help. Don't run away, now."

She stood up. As the candle moved, black shadows crowded round me, and my fear came leaping back.

"Emily! Don't leave me here in the dark! Can't you... can't you just phone somebody?"

"I haven't got a mobile," she said. "My dad won't let me – waste of money, he says. Anyway, it wouldn't be any good down here, would it?"

"Jenny's got a phone," I said. "She's outside."

"All right, I'll get Jenny to call for help."

She started to move away, and the light began to fade. I couldn't help it – I started to whimper with fear.

Emily must have heard me. She said, "I'll leave the candle here – I've got another one. Look, I'll tell Jenny and then I'll come back as quick as I can. All right?"

"Yes," I said in a small voice. "Thanks, Emily."

I heard her footsteps dying slowly away. There was still a small glow from the candle, which she must have left near the edge of the hole. The light didn't reach down to me, but at least it was something to look at. It took my mind off the dark, the stillness, the cold.

Where was Emily? Surely she should have been back by now. But maybe – maybe she would never come back. She'd go home as if nothing had happened, and leave me here for days and days, starving and thirsty, all alone.

No! Don't think about scary things. Look at the light, not the shadows. Think about God holding you in the palm of his hand.

What was that? Footsteps! She was coming back!

"You OK down there?"

"Yes. Glad you came back, though."

"Jenny rang 999. They're going to send out the Mountain Rescue team."

"H-how long do you think that will take?"

"I don't know. It might be a bit before anyone comes. Look, I'm going to blow out one candle. We might need it later."

The shadows crawled closer, and I shivered.

"Are - are there any rats living here? Or bats?"

"Not that I've ever seen."

"Do you come here a lot? But why?"

"Mind your own business," she said sharply. "You know, you've really messed me up, Dense. Why'd you have to poke your nose in? This used to be my place that nobody knew about. Now it'll be all round the village and I'll never be able to come here again."

"Sorry."

There was a long, chilly silence. Water dripped somewhere far away.

I tried again. "I really am sorry, Emily. It wasn't... I didn't mean to mess you around, I just wanted to ask you something. About the ghost. Was it..." I stopped, took a deep breath. "Was it really you all the time?"

"Me? You're joking. You think I would stand there moaning and groaning and rattling chains, just to give you a fright? I've got better things to do."

"Moaning and rattling? But... is that what you thought it sounded like? It wasn't like that at all." I couldn't remember just what I had told her, probably not very much.

"What did it sound like then?" she said curiously.

"It sounded to me like... somebody crying... in the cupboard."

"Oh," she said.

That was all, but it was like seeing a hairline crack in the wall of a dam. Sooner or later, you know the dam will burst.

Another long silence. I waited.

"You're right," she said at last. "It was me."

CHAPTER 17

TRAPPED

"But what had you done?"

"Oh, nothing much," she said wearily. "The last time it was because I didn't clean my shoes properly, he said."

"You mean to say they locked you in a cupboard, just for that?"

"Not they. Him. It's nothing to do with Mum – she tries to stop him. Then he hits her too."

"Does he hit you?"

"Yeah, but Mum gets the worst of it."

"What a pig!" I said fiercely. "Why does your mum put up with it? She could leave – she could get a divorce."

"She doesn't want to," said Emily. "I've asked her, more than once."

"Why not?"

"Says she still loves him." Her voice was flat and hopeless. "I suppose he's OK sometimes – when he's not in one of his moods. You can see them coming on, those moods. You sort of tiptoe round him. You try not to do anything wrong, but it's no good. He always finds something..."

"And then he goes mad?"

"Sometimes I think he *is* mad. I mean, *really* crazy, like. He sort of can't stop himself... and then, next day, he'll be all right again. As if nothing had happened."

"You should do something," I said. "Tell somebody – ring up that children's help line – there must be *something* you can do!"

"Mum said..." She stopped.

"What?"

"I shouldn't be telling you any of this!" she cried. "Mum said to keep my mouth shut, never tell anybody, or they'd put him away! And I'd be put in care, and I might never see her again."

I said quickly, "I won't tell. I won't breathe a word – promise."

Don't cry, Emily – oh, please don't cry!

I wanted to hold her hand, comfort her somehow, but I couldn't reach her, trapped where I was. I suddenly saw that she was trapped too. The difference was, I had a chance of being rescued.

"If I was you," I said, "I would run away from home."

She said, "I think about it – all the time. But I can't. I've got nowhere to go to."

"Nobody at all? No relatives or nothing?"

"I have got an auntie, but I haven't seen her for years. Aunt Gina. She used to come and stay when I was little. But Dad had a row with her and said she was never to come back. I had a doll she gave me – he put her in the bin."

"He does sound charming, your dad."

She said, "Sometimes I pretend he's not my dad at all, just my stepfather. And my real dad will turn up one day and then everything will be all right – happy ever after... all that stuff." She laughed fiercely.

"Maybe it's true. I don't see how he could be so horrible to you, if he really was your dad."

"When I was younger he wasn't so bad. Or maybe I was better at doing what he said. I dunno. Seems like as I get older, he gets worse. And the really scary thing..."

She hesitated.

"Yes?"

"Shhh! Thought I heard someone coming."

We listened hard. Silence, as dead as the tomb of Pharaoh.

I felt cold now right through to my bones. It was hard to stop my teeth chattering. I thought of hot chocolate... bowls of hot soup...

"Denise, are you all right? Don't go to sleep. Denise!"

"I'm OK. A b-bit cold, that's all."

"Here, you can have my coat. I don't need it – I can walk about and keep warm." She lowered it down by one sleeve, and I caught it as it fell.

"Thanks, Emily. D-don't know what I'd have done if you weren't here... I'll remember you in my will. You can have all my jewels and my priceless art collection."

I heard her walking up and down the tunnel for a bit. I was thinking I would have to find a new name for her. Deadly Emily didn't seem to suit her, not now.

When she came back to check up on me, I said, "What were you starting to say, before, about something scary?"

"Oh, well... My mum's going into hospital soon, for an operation on her stomach."

"Is it serious?"

"Yes, but she's not... not likely to die or anything."

"So what's the scary bit?"

She said in a low voice, "I'm scared of being on my own with Dad. He's never really hurt me before – she always stopped him. But when she's in hospital..."

"Come and stay with us," I said quickly. "My mum won't mind."

"He would never let me. He'd say the neighbours would think it was odd."

"We *are* the neighbours," I said.

"Oh, you know what I mean. I just know he'd never let me."

"When does your mum have to go in?"

"Pretty soon. Could be any time. She's waiting to hear from the hospital."

"What are you going to do?"

"I don't know." She sounded defeated. "Before you came along, I thought I might come and stop here – just while Mum's away. I've got a sleeping bag and enough tins of food to last about a week, and loads of candles."

"Ugh! I couldn't live down here for a week. No way. Too cold and dark."

"I'm not scared of the dark. I'm used to it now," she said bitterly.

I said, "I know somewhere much better. Trouble is, it's a long way away."

"Where?"

"In London. My old house – nobody lives there, the owner's abroad. Ages ago I had this plan worked out, using the prize from the art competition – but I've lost that..."

"Have you?"

"Yes. I think I must have dropped it going home."

A short pause. Then she said all in a rush, "You didn't drop it, I nicked it. I'm sorry. You can have it back now..."

"No, keep it. I don't need it any more – you do. It will get you to London."

"London!" She sounded quite panicky – strange, when she didn't mind the thought of living down a mine. "I've never been there in my life. How would I ever find your house?"

I thought for a moment.

"How about if I went too?"

"You don't really mean that," she said.

"Yes I do. I owe you, don't I? You helped me, so I'll help you. I promise."

She said, "I bet you forget all about this as soon as we get out of here."

"Oh yeah? How much do you bet? Listen, we could really do it. We could. I know exactly how."

"Go on."

"We pretend we're going to school as usual, right? We get the bus to Caston, then we use those tickets to go to London by train. At school they'll think we're off sick. We'll have all day before anyone knows we're missing."

"Is that long enough to get to London?"

"Of course it is. It's only about four hours on the train, plus another hour to get across London to my place. Now then, what are we going to need?"

"Money. Food."

"Food? There are shops in London, you know. But money – how much have you got?"

"Not much," she said. "I've got some in the savings bank, but I can't get it out unless Mum signs for it."

I said, "I've got quite a bit. I was saving up to buy an iPod, but this is more important."

"I'll pay you back afterwards," she said quickly.

"How long will you want to stay there?" I asked.

"I dunno. A week – two weeks, maybe. I'll write down the hospital number, then I can ring them to ask when Mum's coming out."

"Good idea. Hey, we'll need something else – clothes to change into. We can't go around in our school clothes. And we'd better take an A to Z."

"A to Z? What's that?"

"A book with maps of the whole of London. In case we get lost."

"Thought you said you knew your way around London."

"Bits of it I do, yes. Other bits I haven't got a clue about."

She hesitated. "I don't know if I want to do this. It all sounds too risky."

"It'll be easy," I said. "You wait and see."

"I don't like big cities much."

"That's because you've never been to London. You'll like London. I'll show you all the sights."

"London – for the time of your life!" she said. And she laughed.

***

"Hallo-o! Anybody there?"

"Yes! Yes! We're here!"

Suddenly the place was filled with shouts, hurrying feet, and lights so bright they hurt my eyes.

"Don't worry, lass, we'll have you out in no time."

"Any bones broken?"

"Lucky she landed where she did. She could have fallen twice as far."

"Up you get, lass. Eh, you're as light as a feather. Up she comes!"

As they lifted me up on the stretcher, I looked around for Emily. I wanted to thank her, but she'd vanished without even saying goodbye.

CHAPTER 18

THE LONG ROAD HOME

"Never thought it would be this easy," said Emily.

We were on the London train, heading south at 80 miles an hour. It was much swifter and smoother than the coach. I liked it. We ought to be in London by two o'clock, long before anyone noticed we were missing.

And when they did notice? I was feeling bad about that. Mum would go absolutely crazy. I had left a note by the teapot, saying I'd gone away for a few days, I hadn't been kidnapped, I was perfectly safe. But it probably wouldn't do much good – she would still worry. And still be very angry.

After the mine episode she was so furious I thought she was about to catch fire. "I *told* you never to go near the place. I told you it was dangerous. And what do you do? You go right in and get yourself half-killed, and if Jenny hadn't got more sense you'd have dragged her in too." Then she rang Dad and I got another roasting from him, and no pocket money for weeks.

Emily didn't get into trouble - quite the opposite. "LOCAL HEROINE IN MINE DRAMA" was all over the front page of the Caston News. Her parents were so pleased with her, it seemed they never got around to asking her why she was there in the first place.

Fortunately I was off school while all the fuss was going on. I had sprained my ankle so badly that I couldn't put my foot to the ground.

Emily came to see me once. We talked about nothing very much, until she said all at once, "My mum got a letter today. From the hospital."

"What did it say?"

"Two weeks on Monday."

We looked at each other.

"Did you mean what you said, back then?" she asked.

"Yes, of course."

"But what about your foot?"

"It'll just have to be better by then."

***

I shouldn't have done it. I know that now. Running away was stupid and dangerous and it caused even more problems - don't ever try it. All I can say is, I thought at the time that it was the right thing to do. I was loving my enemy. I was keeping a promise.

I never even thought of asking God what I should do. If I had, things could have been different. We could have tried to solve the problem, not run away from it.

But secretly, of course, I wanted to run away. I thought it would be fun.

How wrong can you be?

***

My ankle was a lot better, though not perfect. I couldn't walk very far without wanting to rest it. So why was I taking my games kit to school? Answer: the bag held not games kit but some spare clothes, a London A to Z, and all the money I possessed.

At the school bus stop everyone else got off as usual, but Emily and I stayed put. No one seemed to notice except the driver.

"Not going to school today, love? That'll help the accident statistics."

Emily muttered something about a dentist's appointment.

We got out at the railway station. The ticket office was shut, so we went straight onto the platform. A ten-minute wait for the local train, a change at Allenbury, and there we were on the main line train, speeding towards London. Nobody had questioned us; nobody had spoken to us at all.

When we felt hungry we got a snack from the buffet car. Emily looked out at the rushing landscape. "Bit flat, isn't it? No hills, no stone walls... I've never been this far south before."

"It's not the South Pole," I said. "It's actually quite civilised."

"Tickets, please!"

Emily got out the famous white envelope and showed the man the travel voucher. It was plain he didn't like the look of it.

"What's this supposed to be, then?"

"Our ticket."

"This here is not a ticket. This here should have been exchanged at the booking office for a proper ticket. I can't accept this!"

"The booking office was shut," I said. "What were we supposed to do, sit there until it opened, middle of next week sometime?"

"Cheeky young madam. What are your parents thinking about, letting you loose on your own? They want their heads seeing to."

"My parents are divorced," I said as mournfully as I could. "My dad lives in London. I hardly ever see him now."

"Well, I hope he's got the sense to meet you at the other end, that's all. Kids like you aren't safe to be let loose." He went off, muttering to himself.

"Phew! I thought he was going to chuck us off the train."

"So did I. Probably while it was still moving."

At long last the train came smoothly to a halt. "London Euston. All change!"

Fortunately no one was checking tickets at the barrier. We stood in the huge station, watching people hurry about. Everyone seemed to know where they were going.

"It's like an ant heap when you poke it with a stick," said Emily.

"Oh, this isn't even busy. You should see it at rush hour." I was trying to sound confident and streetwise. Actually I'd have given a million pounds for the sight of Dad's face in the crowd.

"Where do we go now?" Emily asked.

Aha! I spotted something nearly as welcome as a familiar face: the Underground sign. We got our tickets and followed the directions to the Northern Line.

At the top of a long escalator, Emily hung back. "Do we have to go down there?"

"You're not scared, are you? Emily Smith, heroine of the mine? You ought to love the Underground."

"Well I don't. I don't like it – the noise and the crowds. And the smell!"

"Look, Emily, I don't know any other way to get there. A taxi would cost a bomb – and the taxi driver might remember where we went."

"Can't we walk?"

"You don't understand. London's huge. It would be like walking from Brilby to Caston and back."

"All right then," said Emily. But she stepped onto the escalator as if she was going over Niagara Falls. And when at last we came up again at Clapham, her face was so pale she might have been underground for months.

"Nearly there," I said. "It's just a bus ride now."

We were both starving, so we got a takeaway pizza and ate it at the bus stop. By now schoolchildren were in the streets going home. Tom would be wondering why I wasn't on the bus in Caston. The sooner we got under cover, the better.

At last we were walking up Dorset Avenue. There was number 12, looking just the same as ever. I marched up the steps and rang the bell. "Just checking..."

"What will you say if somebody comes?"

But the house was quite silent. The street seemed asleep in the afternoon sun. I don't think anyone saw us slip through the gate at the side of the house. Now came the moment of truth. Would the key still be there?

It was – hanging on its secret hook under the lowest shelf in the shed. ("Don't tell Dad. He thinks it would be a security risk," Mum had said long ago.)

We let ourselves in by the back door. The house had a musty, dusty smell, like Gran's attic. The stale air felt as if it had sat there undisturbed for months.

I wanted to open all the windows, but Emily stopped me. "People might notice," she said.

"This is London, not Brilby. Nobody takes much notice of anybody else. But maybe you're right... we'd better be a bit careful. Keep the curtains drawn. Not show lights at night."

Emily flicked a switch. "That'll be easy – there's no electricity."

"It's probably turned off at the mains. It's OK, I've seen Dad do it."

I opened the understairs cupboard. There was a switch in there somewhere, and a way to turn the water on too – pretty vital, that. I didn't fancy living in a house where you couldn't flush the loo.

Success! We had lights and water. The next thing was food. There were a few tins in the kitchen cupboards, but we both agreed not to touch them. Breaking and entering was bad enough without stealing as well.

"I'll get some things from that shop we passed on the corner," Emily offered.

I nodded. It was better that I didn't show my face there – Gita, who had been at my old school, might start asking questions.

Anyway I was quite glad just to sit there, resting my bad ankle on the sofa (an enormous thing in shiny black leather, far too big for the room). There was a lot of new furniture, which made our old carpets and curtains look extremely tatty, but no ornaments, no photos, no magazines. You could tell the place was nobody's real home.

It was then that I realised this wasn't my home either. How ridiculous! I was feeling homesick again. Homesick, that is, for Brilby.

CHAPTER 19

CHANGE OF ADDRESS

That evening (after a strange meal of corned beef sandwiches, Rice Krispies and Mars Bars), I decided to phone Mum. I had no mobile – I'd have to use a public phone.

Just on the off chance I tried the phone in the house. Amazing! It seemed to be working. For a second or two I heard the ringing tone at the other end...

"Hey! What are you doing?" Emily shouted.

"Ringing Mum."

She snatched the phone out of my hand and slammed it down.

I said, "What d'you do that for? I just want to let her know we're OK, that we'll be back soon. I wasn't going to tell her anything..."

"You idiot! Don't you know they can trace phone calls these days and find out where you rang from? I've seen it on the telly."

"Oh."

"And anyway, what was that about going back soon?"

"But I thought... when your mum gets out of hospital..."

"Oh well, you go back if you want to. But I've decided. I'm never going back – not ever."

I stared at her. "But Emily! What will you live on when all the money's gone? And what if the owner of the house comes back?"

"Then I'll get a cardboard box and live in the streets. I've seen that on the telly too... Or else I'll try and find my auntie."

"Your auntie? Do you know where she lives?"

Emily unfolded a scrap of paper from her bag. "Gina White, 43 Sheppard House, Kensington Park Road. I copied it out of Mum's address book. Mind you, I don't know if she still lives there – I haven't seen her since I was seven."

"Yeah, you said. Your dad quarrelled with her and said she could never come back, right?"

"She was really nice. I bet she would help me, if I could find her."

I looked in the A to Z. "It's over Notting Hill way. We could go tomorrow. Want to?"

***

It was a long bus ride to Notting Hill. I knew how to get there because I'd been to the Carnival a couple of times. Using the A to Z we found Kensington Park Road, no trouble. But where was Sheppard House?

We walked up and down twice without finding it. At last we asked a postman who was emptying a letter box.

"Sheppard House? There's no Sheppard House in Kensington Park Road. I should know, it was on my walk for years. Sure you got the right street?"

I checked the index of the A to Z. There was no other Kensington Park Road in the whole of London.

"Could you have copied it down wrong?" I said.

"Suppose so. Mum's writing is a bit scribbly. Can't go back and check it now though, can I?"

It was a hot, sticky day. I got some ice cream to try and cheer her up, but that only left us feeling stickier. All at once I found myself longing for a breath of cool wind from the moors.

"Is it always this hot in London?" Emily grumbled.

"Well, at least it isn't raining. I bet it's raining in Brilby right now."

On the bus going back, she went on about how awful London was. Miles and miles of nothing but buildings... millions of cars... nothing green...

We were passing Hyde Park at the time. "If you think that's not green, you need your eyes tested," I said.

"But it's tiny. I can see the buildings at the other side. And there are people all over it. Where do you go if you want to get away from people?"

Of course I felt I had to stick up for London. We almost had a quarrel. We were both fed up and my ankle was hurting again. But then, as we walked home from the bus stop, something happened to take our minds right off London versus Brilby.

We were passing an electrical shop in the High Road. I glanced at the window, where a TV set was switched on.

"Emily! That's us!"

There we were, side by side on the screen. It was the photo that had been taken for the Caston News. Not a very good one: Emily trying to look heroic, me looking embarrassed. For a second or two we stood there, hypnotised.

Emily tugged my arm. "Come on! We'd better get indoors double quick."

"Yes. We'll go the back way, it's quieter."

I led her along the narrow alleyway that ran past the end of our garden. The back gate squealed nastily as if on purpose. But no one was there to hear.

Emily switched on the 24-hour news channel. We didn't have long to wait before our faces filled the screen again.

"Police are trying to trace two schoolgirls who have been missing for the last 36 hours. They were last seen on the school bus in Caston, near Allenbury, but they never attended school that day. It's thought they may have travelled to London, possibly by train."

"That ticket collector," said Emily. "I bet he remembered us."

A policeman was talking now. "It may simply be that the girls have run away from home. But there have been two other recent cases of children going missing in the Allenbury area. These girls may be in danger – we're making every effort to find them."

The newsreader said, "The mother of one of the girls is in hospital recovering from a serious operation. She has not yet been told that her daughter is missing. The other mother made this appeal..."

Oh no! It was Mum! I could hardly bear to watch.

"Emily, if you're watching this, please, please let us know you're OK. I won't be angry, I promise. Just ring me. I need to know if you're all right..." I could tell she was trying not to cry.

"I'm going to ring her," I said, standing up.

"No! Not from here! Do it from a public phone."

"But that means going out again. That's risky too."

"Well don't ring her. Didn't you say you'd left her a letter, anyway?"

"She can't have found it," I said wretchedly.

We had a long argument. In the end we decided we would wait for dusk, and then go out to find a public phone. "Dusk – not dark," I said. "You get some dodgy characters round here after dark. You know... kerb-crawlers."

"What are kerb-crawlers?"

"Men that drive around in their cars trying to pick girls up. Denise and I got followed all the way from the swimming pool once – it was really creepy."

"What happened?"

"Nothing. But after that, her mum or my mum always came to meet us."

Waiting for the time to pass, we had another peculiar meal – Rice Krispies again, crisps and peanut butter toast.

"I hate peanut butter," I said.

"You do the shopping next time, then."

At last, when the shadows had crept right across the street, we slipped out again. We had plenty of change for the phone, but the first one we came to only took cards and the second one was out of order. In the next one a fat woman was jabbering away. Now and then she gave us a funny look, as if we reminded her of someone.

"I don't like the look of her," said Emily suddenly. "Let's go back."

The fat lady was still watching us as we turned the corner.

It was nearly dark in our back alley. Suddenly I stopped – something was wrong.

"The house! We didn't leave it like that, did we?"

Every light in the house was on, from kitchen to attic. Yellow light streamed out across the dark garden.

"Oh, no!"

"The owners have come back," said Emily.

"Or else... I suppose Mum might have given the police this address. Told them to search the place. Come on, let's get out of here!"

"But all our things..."

"We'll have to leave them. At least we've got the money. Come on!"

We ran back down the alley. What were we going to do now? I had no idea.

"Homeless in London," said Emily. "Where do we find a cardboard box?"

CHAPTER 20

SOMEWHERE TO HIDE

Where the alley met the lighted street, we stopped. Neither of us wanted to venture out.

"Now what?" said Emily.

"I don't know. We can't hang around here, though. If they've found our things, they might start searching the whole area."

I thought hard. The Common... no, too dark and dangerous. Denise's house wouldn't be safe either, for quite a different reason – Denise's mum would want to send us straight home to Brilby. (Have you noticed, grown-ups always stick together?) And my dad would be just as bad... anyway, I wasn't at all sure I could remember where he lived.

"We could get on a bus," I said.

"Where to?"

"Anywhere – first one that comes. We need to get out of here sharpish."

I could see she didn't think much of the idea. But she didn't have a better one.

There was no one at the bus stop. In fact there were not many people around at all. A couple of passers-by gave us looks that meant, "Why aren't you in bed by now?"

The air was turning chilly. I had only a thin jacket, and Emily didn't have one at all – hers was back at the house. She hopped from foot to foot, trying to keep warm.

"I could murder a bag of chips," she said.

"We'd better not spend any more than we have to. How much have you got left?"

Before she could answer, a car pulled up beside us and the driver got out. "Excuse me, girls. Don't suppose you can tell me how to get to Clapham Common?"

I gave him directions as well as I could. For some reason I had the impression that he wasn't really listening. His eyes flicked from me to Emily and back again.

"Thank you. That's very helpful. Now why don't I give you a lift home? It's late. I don't like to see young girls out on their own as late as this."

"No thanks. I'm not allowed to take lifts with strangers."

"Well, that's sensible of you. But it's not very sensible to be stranded at a bus stop, waiting for a bus that may never come. Your mum must be getting worried by now. Just hop in and I'll take you straight home." He opened the passenger door.

"I said no. Go away!"

"We don't need your lift," said Emily. "The bus is coming."

"Only trying to help..."

"Leave us alone or I'll scream!" I said loudly.

For a moment he seemed to hesitate. Then he got quickly into his car and drove away – up a side street, not at all in the direction of Clapham.

Emily said, "That was a bit over the top, wasn't it? 'Leave us alone or I'll scream!'"

"I don't think so. Better safe than sorry... Here's the bus."

It said ELEPHANT AND CASTLE on the front of the bus. I had only the vaguest idea where that was, and no idea what to do when we got there.

"We were crazy to do this," I said. "Absolutely mad."

"We didn't have any choice."

"No, I meant crazy to run away in the first place."

"You want to go back, don't you?" she said. "Go then. I'll be OK."

"Not on your own in London, you won't. I'm not going back unless you come too."

"It's all very well for you," she said bitterly. "You'd get a bit of a telling-off maybe. Naughty girl, slap wrist, don't do it again. But me – my dad would half-kill me. That's why I'm not going back."

There was nothing I could say. I stared out at the endlessly unrolling streets; darkened shops, lighted houses; street lights, headlights, chip shops, pubs; empty night beyond park fences – and no place anywhere for Emily and me.

Oh God, I'm sorry. I shouldn't be here – I've messed things up yet again. What do I do now? Show me what to do, please, please, please...

Emily nudged me. "Oi, wake up."

"I wasn't asleep."

"Yes you were."

"Wasn't. I just had my eyes closed."

"What for? Saying your prayers?"

I hesitated – she would laugh. "Yeah, that's right."

"Ourfatherwhichartinheavenharoldbethyname," she gabbled. "We need a place to stay and a hundred pounds. No, make that five hundred pounds. Then we won't need to bother you again for a week or two."

I said nothing, and she looked at me curiously. "You don't really believe in that stuff?" she said.

"Why shouldn't I?"

"Because it's a load of rubbish, that's why. There's nobody out there. It's a waste of time."

"How do you know there's nobody there? You only think that – you can't prove it. Anyway, I've prayed for things and they did happen... sometimes."

"Like when?"

"Like down the mine..." I stopped. I couldn't find the words to talk about that moment when I felt so near to God.

"What are you on about? That wasn't God helping you – that was me, remember? Me. Emily Smith. A human being."

"That wasn't what I..."

"You know, I nearly didn't bother," she said, grinning. "I was so angry with you for following me, I nearly went off and left you there. Teach you a lesson, I thought."

"Oh, great, thanks. But what made you change your mind?"

"I dunno. I heard you shouting for a while, then it all went quiet. And I sort of began to imagine how I would feel if it happened to me... So then I came to look for you."

I stared at her. *Do to others as you would have them do to you* – she had been doing that, hadn't she? But who had put the idea into her mind? Who had helped her feel sorry for me, her worst enemy? If that wasn't an answer to prayer then nothing was.

The bus stopped at a traffic light – and I saw something. If the lights had changed a second quicker I'd have missed it altogether.

"Emily! Did you see that?"

"What?"

"That street name back there. Kennington Park Road."

"So?"

"Your aunt's address – are you sure it was Kensington, not Kennington Park Road?"

"Oh – right! I get you. Worth a try, isn't it?"

We shot off the bus at the next stop.

"Sheppard House. Sheppard House. Sounds like a block of flats or something." The darkness made it hard to read names and numbers. We walked along slowly; my ankle was hurting again.

A police car went cruising past, and we ducked into the shadows.

"Think they saw us?"

"Don't be daft," I said. "You think every police force in the country is on red alert looking for us two? Have you taken up bank robbery on the quiet?"

"We might need to soon. When the money runs out."

"Oh, oh. Is that them coming back?"

The police car had done a U-turn at the next lights. It was coming back on our side of the road. I still don't know if they had actually noticed us, but they certainly noticed Emily when she burst from the shadows and sprinted down the road.

"Come on!" she shouted, and I followed her. What else could I do? She swerved down an alley too narrow for a car. Behind us I heard the squeal of brakes and the slam of a car door.

The alley ended in an open space. Big estate, blocks of flats, parked cars...

"In here!" Emily panted. We slid through a tiny gap between two huge wheelie bins. It was totally dark behind there, and it smelled so disgusting I wished I could stop breathing.

For a while we heard footsteps and voices, but then they died away. Emily peered through the gap between the bins, and suddenly she clutched my arm.

"See!" she whispered. "Sheppard House – we found it!"

Actually the sign said SH PPARD HO SE. It was written on a tall block of flats not far away. Oh, thank God! Now we would be safe.

Cautiously we crossed the open ground. A sign told us that Flat 43 was on the 11th floor. There was a lift, but the notice on the door said OUT OF ORDER. Various rude messages were scribbled on this.

It took us ages to climb the stairs; I mean it took me ages, because of my ankle. Emily danced about impatiently, one floor above. At last we reached the 11th floor and found a narrow hallway with several doors.

Emily knocked loudly at number 43. Nobody answered.

"Maybe she's in bed." She knocked even louder, but nothing happened.

Disappointment hit us both like a ton weight of solid granite. I slid down onto the floor and just sat there with my back to the wall. Now what?

"Wonder if she still lives here? I'll ask next door."

She knocked. After a minute a woman opened the door on a chain.

"Yeah? What d'you want?"

"Sorry to bother you," said Emily in her best smarmy-polite voice, "but do you happen to know if Gina White still lives at number 43?"

"Far as I know she does."

"Is she away?"

"Nah, she'll be at work. She's a barmaid. She'll be back when the pubs shut."

"Where does she work?" I asked.

"I dunno, do I? Some pub near the Elephant. Hey, who are you, anyway? Do I know you from somewhere?"

"Don't think so. Come on, we'd better go." I heaved myself up off the floor.

"I do know you. You're the two kids that was on the telly just now – the runaways! Oi, wait!"

We ran for the stairs. Oh, no... eleven flights down. Eleven times 16 concrete steps. And every one of them punished my ankle.

"Come on! Come on! I bet she's ringing the police right now!"

"Don't wait for me... you go on..."

"Just get a move on, will you?"

It was endless. It was like a nightmare. Down and round... down and round... surely we must be halfway now... Landing four. Landing three. What was that outside the frosted glass? Was it the glow of a flashing blue light?

I could hear voices below, and feet pounding on the stairs. Emily turned back in panic. "Quick! Find a place to hide!" But this landing was like all the others: an empty space with four doors, all shut.

She went charging past me, up the stairs again. I tried to follow her, but my strength was giving out. Halfway up the next flight I sank down exhausted.

"Here's one of them!" Somebody grabbed me. "And where's your friend, eh?"

I didn't answer. Up above, higher and higher, the sound of her footsteps faded away.

CHAPTER 21

CHANGE PLACES

"You can let go of me," I said. "I'm not going anywhere – I can't, I've hurt my foot."

The policewoman gave me a doubtful look. But she let me sit down on the stairs.

"Your friend isn't going anywhere either. At least, she'll have to stop when she gets to the top. Now which one are you – Emily Smith or Emily Smith?"

I said nothing, and she sighed.

"Look, you may not believe this, but we're on your side. We know you're not criminals. But you are a bit young to be wandering around London on your own, aren't you?"

I nodded. Actually I was quite relieved to be caught. No more running, no more hiding... But what about Emily? A policeman had followed her up the stairs. Had he caught up with her yet?

"What will happen now? Will we have to go home?"

"Is that so terrible?"

"Not for me. But it is for Emily."

"Why?"

"I'm not allowed to say."

There was a sudden crackle from the radio she wore. A voice said something urgent that I couldn't understand.

"What's the matter?" But she was listening and didn't answer me.

"What is it? Is it Emily?"

She said, "Your friend Emily has got out on the roof. She's threatening to jump. Is it likely that she means it?"

Horrified, I whispered, "I don't know. She did say – she did say she was never going home..."

***

It was cold up there. A chill wind blew in through the open doorway at the top of the stairs.

I was gasping as if I'd just climbed Everest without oxygen. The policewoman had half-helped, half-carried me all the way up. As we neared Floor 11, I remembered Emily's Aunt Gina. We stopped while the policewoman talked on the radio to somebody on the ground.

"If she comes back, they'll send her up here. Will Emily listen to her, do you think?"

"I don't know." I didn't know if she would listen to me, either.

Far below I heard the wail of an ambulance. "Just a precaution," said the policewoman, but she hurried me on.

The policeman who had followed Emily was at the top of the stairs, looking out at the roof. "She's still there. Says she'll jump if we go any closer."

"How did she get out?"

He pointed to a broken padlock that swung from the door. It looked as if it had been vandalised ages ago.

"Right, kid. We've got help coming but it won't get here straight away. Think you can help us talk her away from the edge?"

I looked out. The roof was as flat as a table top, with only a waist-high rail around the edge. All the lights of London were spread out below: red lights on other tall buildings; moving lights in the streets far below; a dark strip that must be the river; and another dark shadow in the shape of a person.

She was right by the rail. Her face was turned towards us. She looked like a hunted fox with nowhere else to run.

"Emily. Are you OK?" What an idiotic question, I thought as soon as I said it.

"I'm not going back!" she shouted. "Never! I'd rather be dead!"

"Maybe you won't have to." I tried to sound calm, soothing. "Maybe you could stay with your aunt. Why don't you come and talk to her?"

"Where is she? Let me see her."

"Not here yet. But they'll bring her up here as soon as she gets back."

Behind me I could hear the policewoman talking on her radio. I looked at her questioningly. She shook her head.

Surely Aunt Gina must come back soon. The pubs must be shut by now. Then I imagined her going to a friend's after work and not coming home at all. She would read in tomorrow's paper about the death of a girl called Emily Smith, and think, "How sad. Same name as my niece, too."

Oh God, please help me. You did it before; please do it again. Just one more time. Help me! Tell me the right things to say!

My mind was empty. At random I said, "Emily, I wish you'd move away from the edge a bit. You're making me nervous – I hate heights."

After a moment she did move, grudgingly, a couple of steps away from the railing. But she was still close enough to be over it in two seconds if anyone threatened her.

The cold wind blew across the roof, straight from Siberia. Emily hugged her arms to her chest. No jacket – she must be freezing.

"Can I lend her my jacket?"

"OK. You're not going out there, though. I'll throw it."

"Want my jacket, Emily? Here it comes."

The policeman threw it, but it landed short, lying in a heap a few paces away from her. I felt him grow tense, judging the distance... "Don't risk it!" I muttered. "She's very quick. You wouldn't have time."

Nobody moved. Then all of a sudden, swift as a bird after food, she darted in, snatched the jacket and was off again.

"Thanks, Denise!" she called.

I said, "Listen, you are not to jump wearing that jacket, it's new. My mum will kill you if you mess it up."

Suddenly I remembered that awful day in the mine. It was repeating itself in a weird kind of way, but we had changed places. And we were high up, not deep down. One thing hadn't altered, though... the fear, as sharp as a knife.

Remember, always remember: from beyond the east to the furthest west, from the heights to the depths... He will be there to lead me; he will be there to help me.

***

Meanwhile, I had half-noticed the policewoman still using her radio. Now she beckoned me further inside the doorway.

"Why is she afraid to go home? Is it her father she's scared of?"

"I— I can't tell you. I promised..."

"Well then, tell me this. We think her dad's done a runner. Should we tell her or not?"

"Done a runner? I don't understand... How do you know?"

She said patiently, "I got my boss to ring the police in... where is it again? Caston? Right. The Caston police wanted to interview Mr Smith – ask him some questions about Emily. But they couldn't find him. He wasn't at work or at home. He hadn't visited his wife in hospital. His car had gone."

"Oh. But are you – are you sure he won't come back?"

"We don't know."

"He might be anywhere. He might have come to London to look for Emily." But somehow I didn't think that was likely. Wouldn't he have told someone – asked for time off work? Not just vanished.

If he really had gone, gone for good, then Emily had nothing to be afraid of. But would she believe it? Would she think it was some kind of trick?

"Emily," I shouted. "Listen - your dad's gone away, nobody knows where. It's all right. It's safe to go home."

"What?"

"Your dad - he's gone away. You can go home!"

I wasn't ready for what happened next. She let out a wild cry. "Denise! You promised! You said you would never tell!" Then she was running to the rail, climbing it...

I charged out of the doorway, shouting something, I don't know what. Halfway across the roof my ankle gave way beneath me, and I fell sprawling. I lay there, face down, all the breath knocked out of me... scared to look up...

At last I did look up. She was still there, sitting astride the rail.

"I didn't... didn't tell..." I gasped. "Only that you didn't want to go home..."

For a minute she didn't reply.

"If he's gone away," she said slowly, "Mum's going to blame me. It'll be all my fault - she'll hate me. So, what is there to go home for?"

She was trembling. She began to lift herself over the rail.

"No! Stop!" I cried. "You don't know - she may be glad he's gone. But if you go too, she'll be left with nobody - all alone."

For a long moment she held herself quite still. She was looking down at the million twinkling lights and the darkness that waited to swallow her up.

Oh, please let her listen! Please let her change her mind!

I gabbled, "It isn't your fault – none of it. It was all *his* fault. Don't let him win in the end!"

"No," she said thoughtfully.

Slowly and carefully, she got down on the inside of the railing. She helped me get up. She seemed quite calm. I felt most peculiar, as if I'd just been underneath a ten-ton truck.

Now the police came out to meet us, a bit cautiously, as if they weren't quite sure it was all over. I remember the policeman putting his jacket round my shoulders. I was freezing.

"I'm tired," I said. "Can we go home now?"

Someone else came out of the doorway at the top of the stairs: a tall woman, breathing hard after the long climb. She had the same red hair as Emily.

"Aunt Gina!" Emily cried, and ran into her arms.

CHAPTER 22

SAFELY HOME

My dad drove us all home to Brilby - Emily, me, and Aunt Gina, who was going to stay with Emily while her mum was still in hospital. That was a month ago, and Mrs Smith is home again, but Aunt Gina is still here. I hope she never goes back. She livens the place up. (Brilby, she says, is about as lively as the South London Crematorium.)

At first I found it hard to believe that she and Mrs Smith were sisters - they seemed such opposites. But these days Mrs Smith is much less nervous and scared. She's had all the door locks changed and says she will never let Emily's dad back in the house.

He seems to have gone for good, though. He took a lot of his things with him, plus most of the money from the bank account. His car turned up in Liverpool. He told the man who bought it that he was going to Ireland. Nobody knows where he is now.

"Why do you think he left?" I asked Mum.

"Seems like he was frightened of being questioned by the police. He must have thought it would all come out about the way he treated his family."

But Emily still can't believe he won't come back. She has nightmares about it.

***

Mum's boyfriend has been coming round a lot. He's nothing special: ordinary-looking, rather quiet, pretty boring in fact. But Mum seems to like him.

She said, "I don't know what I'd have done without him when you went missing, Emily. I think I'd have cracked up completely. But Martin was so good – he kept calming me down, telling me it would all come right in the end..."

"And buying us Chinese takeaways so Mum didn't have to cook," said Tom. "You could have stayed away a bit longer, Emily. I wouldn't have minded. I might have got to try the King Prawn Special."

Gran thinks Martin is wonderful. She kept telling Mum what a good husband he would make, until Mum said, "You marry him then, if you're so keen."

Gran went on and on at me for running away. "I can't believe you could be so daft – giving your poor mother a heart attack, not to mention the rest of us, and nearly getting your friend killed, and wasting police time. They should have locked you up in the cells for a night or two. That would teach you."

I didn't argue back. I knew it would only make her worse. But secretly I thought: *all right, it was a stupid thing to do, but good came out of it. Perhaps even mistakes can turn out all right if we put them in God's hands.*

I rang Denise to tell her all about our disastrous trip to London. She already knew part of the story. She'd seen us on the TV news. "We all prayed for you," she said, "and then in the morning you were on the news again – found."

"Wham! Another prayer answered," I said. "Is that what you think it was like? Let me tell you, it wasn't so simple." And I told her the whole story.

She said, "Ending up right outside Aunt Gina's place – that was incredible. Out of the whole of London..."

"I know. I said to Emily, don't you think someone was looking after us that night? And she said, yeah – the bus company, the police."

Denise is coming to visit in a couple of weeks. Of course it will probably rain every day, but she can't say she hasn't been warned.

I wonder how she'll get on with Emily? The names will be confusing, for a start. Denise, Emily and me – known by Denise as Emily and by Emily as Denise.

Pretty soon, though, Emily's going to have to remember my real name. In September we start at the Senior School, where Tom goes - and whether or not Emily and I are in the same class, I am going to be Emily Smith from then on.

And it's goodbye forever to Mrs Bell! Mum said I should get her a leaving present.

"How about this?" I said. "Gran found it at the back of a cupboard." It was a box of chocolates marked "Best before November 1995".

"Only joking, Mum... only joking."

***

Love your enemies; do good to those who hate you.

I was thinking smugly that it's easy to do that when you haven't any enemies left - and then the letter arrived.

Dad and Paula are getting married at Christmas. How would I like to be a bridesmaid, in a dainty pink dress with lace collar and velvet bows? ("And matching pink sickbag?" said Tom.)

How would I like it? Actually I don't have much choice in the matter, short of running away from home. And I don't intend to do that again, not ever.

Oh, I know, I know. Paula's not an enemy exactly... it's just that I can't stand the sight of her.

At one time I would have enjoyed making plans to spoil her wedding day. (Sneezing powder on her bouquet? Trip her up as she goes to cut the cake... splattt!) But I know better now, don't I? Pity.

Don't think about it. Think about something else. It's Saturday and it's raining again. What am I going to do all day? I know. I'm off next door to see if Emily has any good ideas.

Also by Kathy Lee

The Lost Book Trilogy

Far in the future, the sea has taken over, turning huge mountains into islands and swallowing cities whole. Many of the Ancestors were wiped out, but some humans still struggle on: fishing, hunting, keeping away from things left over from the Old Times. Well, who needs the bad luck?

The Book of Secrets

On the island of Insh More, Jamie leads a simple life, but his friend Rob dreams of more – travelling to the great island city of Embra. However, between Rob and his dream lie dangers that neither he nor Jamie have ever encountered before. Dangers that threaten to kill. Can the book in the seal-skin bag save them?

The Book of Good and Evil

Welcome to the magnificent island city of Embra, full of riches, knowledge and power. But for Jamie, Rob and Ali, the city has very different things in store. War, robbery and treachery follow Jamie wherever he goes, but the book in the seal-skin bag is never far away. Can the words inside save him from certain death?

The Book of Life

A blind beggar from the south brings a mysterious message to the King of Lothian. An old friend needs your help... But the message is the start of a dangerous mission, taking Rob and Jamie far from Embra, to a land of darkness, slavery and death. Will they ever be able to escape? And can they still trust in God, even when he seems far away?

The Book of Secrets
£4.99   978 184427 342 3
The Book of Good and Evil
£4.99   978 184427 368 3
The Book of Life
£4.99   978 184427 369 0

About the author

Kathy Lee has been writing books for over ten years, and this book is the first one she ever wrote. *Deadly Emily* has been revised and updated for the 21st century, but this book was just the start of Kathy's great writing career!

She has written about Phoebe and her worries about her weight, money and French pen friends. She's written about Ancient Rome and the early Christians who lived there and followed Jesus. She's written about a group of girls who are good little church girls, until they leave church... And she's written about the future, Jamie and the God of the Old Times. Here are some of the other books she has written that you can get hold of!

Fabulous Phoebe   No Angel
Phoebe's Fortune   No Means No
Phoebe Finds Her Feet   No Love Lost

A Captive in Rome   The Book of Secrets
Rome in Flames   The Book of Good and Evil
The Edge of the Empire   The Book of Life

To get your hands on these books, go to your local Christian bookshop, or go to www.scriptureunion.org.uk/shop

Kathy was born in Scotland, but moved to Carlisle when she was 12. She wanted to live in the African jungle and study chimpanzees, but she never quite managed to get that far. She met her husband on holiday in Greece, and now they live in Hertfordshire with their three sons. She likes nothing better than to be at the seaside and she loves reading, music, eating and walking the dog.

If you liked *Deadly Emily*, you might like...

Jack and the Wardrobe

By Nicola Jemphrey

How do you cope with a dad who drinks too much and a mum who has run off, and not told you where she is?

Not very well, is the answer for Jack. But that all changes when he walks straight into a wardrobe in the middle of a street. Jack starts to find out about the 'owner' of the wardrobe, CS Lewis, and about his own family. What he learns inspires him to make a drastic decision – one that turns his life upside-down for ever.

Jack and the Wardrobe lets you not only follow Jack's story, but also gives you the chance to find out more about CS Lewis, the man who came up with the wardrobe and the land of Narnia behind its doors!

Jack and the Wardrobe

£4.99   978 184427 269 3

Great books from Scripture Union

Fiction

Jack and the Wardrobe, Nicola Jemphrey £4.99, 978 184427 269 3
The Dangerous Road, Eleanor Watkins £4.99, 978 184427 302 7
Fire By Night, Hannah MacFarlane £4.99, 978 184427 323 2
The Scarlet Cord, Hannah MacFarlane £4.99, 978 184427 370 6

The Lost Book Trilogy

The Book of Secrets, Kathy Lee £4.99, 978 184427 342 3
The Book of Good and Evil, Kathy Lee £4.99, 978 184427 368 3
The Book of Life, Kathy Lee £4.99, 978 184427 369 0

Lifepath Adventures

A Land of Broken Vows, Steve Dixon £4.99, 978 184427 371 3
Hard Rock, Fay Sampson £4.99, 978 184427 372 0
In the Shadow of Idris, Ruth Kirtley £4.99, 978 184427 374 4
Pilgrim, Eleanor Watkins £4.99, 978 184427 373 7

Fiction by Patricia St John

Rainbow Garden £4.99, 978 184427 300 3
Star of Light £4.99, 978 184427 296 9
The Mystery of Pheasant Cottage £4.99, 978 184427 297 6
The Tanglewoods' Secret £4.99, 978 184427 301 0
Treasures of the Snow £5.99, 978 184427 298 3
Where the River Begins £4.99, 978 184427 299 0

Bible and Prayer

The 10 Must Know Stories, Heather Butler £3.99, 978 184427 326 3
10 Rulz, Andy Bianchi £4.99, 978 184427 053 8
Parabulz, Andy Bianchi £4.99, 978 184427 227 3
Massive Prayer Adventure, Sarah Mayers £4.99, 978 184427 211 2

God and you!

No Girls Allowed, Darren Hill and Alex Taylor £4.99, 978 184427 209 9
Friends Forever, Mary Taylor £4.99, 978 184427 210 5

Puzzle books

Bible Codecrackers: Moses, Valerie Hornsby £3.99, 978 184427 181 8
Bible Codecrackers: Jesus, Gillian Ellis £3.99, 978 184427 207 5
Bible Codecrackers: Peter & Paul, Gillian Ellis £3.99, 978 184427 208 2

Available from your local Christian bookshop or from
Scripture Union Mail Order, PO Box 5148, Milton Keynes MLO, MK2 2YX
Tel: 0845 07 06 006 Website: www.scriptureunion.org.uk/shop
All prices correct at time of going to print.